# A Journey through the

# Gospels and Acts

By

Kaye Freeman

"The Christ will suffer and rise from the dead on the third day, and repentance and forgiveness of sins will be preached in his name to all nations, beginning at Jerusalem." Luke 24:46-47

This book is dedicated to my beloved husband, Don Freeman.
Thank you for your patience and love.  I love you so much.

ISBN:   978-1-60402-327-5

Book cover and layout:     John Owen

Editors:  Marilyn Price
          Emily & Caleb Freeman
          Darlene Arkison

Published by:     Train-Up A Child Publishing, L.L.C.
                  PO Box 1122
                  Jenks, OK  74037

Website:          www.trainupstudies.com

## About the Author

Kaye Freeman is a wife and a homeschooling mother. She is a graduate of Oklahoma State University. She and her husband, Don, have two children, Emily and Caleb. Attending Victory Bible Institute, Kaye is a part-time student in the Biblical Studies Program. Additionally, she teaches 7th and 8th grade Bible and writing classes at C.E.A., which is a homeschool co-op.

As a child, Kaye faced physical challenges. By the age of 18, she was undergoing her second heart surgery. At that time, she did not know that God is a healing God and that His plans for her future were for good and not for evil. It wasn't until she was an adult that Kaye discovered this wonderful truth about her Lord and Savior. Now she's determined to teach children and teens everywhere the truth about God through the Train-Up A Child Bible Studies.

Website:     www.trainupstudies.com

# Table of Contents

# Lesson 1

# Introduction to the New Testament

Welcome to this study, *A Journey through the Gospels and Acts.* Over the next 24 lessons, you will study about the life of Christ and His influence on mankind. Meeting Jesus' disciples, who left everything to follow Him, you will discover that Christ dramatically impacted their lives. As you study about the birth of the Christian Church, you will become acquainted with some of the apostles who fervently served God regardless of the consequences.

Throughout this workbook, you will be looking up verses in the Bible. If an (OT) follows the verse, it is found in the Old Testament. If an (NT) follows the verse, it is found in the New Testament. Let's get started!

The first order of business is an overall introduction to the New Testament. The Bible is divided into two parts, the Old Testament and the New Testament. While the Old Testament was written before Jesus' life on earth, the New Testament was written after His life on earth. The New Testament is a compilation of 27 books written by approximately eight men. It is divided into four groups of books, which include five historical books, thirteen Pauline epistles, eight general epistles, and a prophetic book, outlining end-time events.

Open your Bible to the Table of Contents located at the front of the book. There you will find a breakdown of the Old and New Testaments with a listing of the books contained in each. Glancing over the New Testament listing, answer the following question by writing your answer in the spaces provided.

1.     List the first five books of the New Testament.

_____     _____     _____

_____     _____

The first four books of the New Testament are known as the Gospels. Gospel means "good news." These books are referred to as such because the writers described the good news of salvation made possible by Jesus' life, death and victorious resurrection. Matthew, Mark, Luke and John wrote the four Gospels.

The book of Acts contains historical data concerning the outpouring of the Holy Spirit and the birth of the Christian Church. Additionally, Acts records the work of the apostles after Jesus' ascension back to the Father in heaven. Luke penned Acts.

**2.** Turning again to the Table of Contents, list the next thirteen books, which are referred to as the Pauline epistles, contained in the New Testament.

_____ _____ _____

_____ _____ _____

_____ _____ _____

_____ _____ _____

_____

The apostle Paul wrote the thirteen Pauline epistles. Romans, 1st and 2nd Corinthians, Galatians, Ephesians, Philippians, Colossians and 1st and 2nd Thessalonians were written to churches. First and 2nd Timothy and Titus were letters to pastors. Philemon was a wealthy slave owner to whom Paul wrote regarding forgiveness and restoration. Concerned about the body of Christ, Paul penned his advice and exhortations in order to prevent believers from falling away from God. Paul's story is an exciting transformation from one who persecuted Christians to a man who willingly put his own life on the line countless times in order to further God's kingdom. You will have the opportunity to read about some of Paul's experiences throughout this study.

Take another look at the New Testament Table of Contents. Answer the question that follows.

**3.** List the next group of epistles, which are referred to as the general epistles. There are eight of them.

_____ \_\_\_\_\_   _____   _____

_____   _____   _____

_____   _____

Hebrews, James, 1st and 2nd Peter, 1st, 2nd and 3rd John and Jude comprise the general epistles. Most biblical scholars agree that Paul wrote the book of Hebrews although there is no solid evidence of this. The remaining books bear the names of their authors. Next to Paul, John, who penned the Gospel of John, 1st, 2nd and 3rd John and Revelation, wrote the greatest number of New Testament books. After taking one last look at the Table of Contents, answer the following question.

**4.** In the following space, write the last book of the New Testament,

which is a prophetic book, outlining end-time events. _____

Considered one of the most difficult books in the New Testament to comprehend, the book of Revelation reveals the three enthronements of Jesus. The first of which is His enthronement in Heaven, where He presently sits at the right-hand of God. His second enthronement will be on the earth during His Millennial reign. This will occur after the Tribulation but before the final judgment of man. Jesus' third enthronement will be in the new heaven and earth, which God will create after the final doom of Satan and the judgment of man.

As you can see, the New Testament is full of good news, excitement and revelation. Is it any wonder that the Bible continually makes the Top 10 best selling book list each year? Over the weeks to come, you are certain to experience Jesus in a way that you have never before experienced Him. As you do, He will prepare you for the exciting calling He has on your life. God bless you as you seek Him.

That's enough for today. Let's review what you've learned:

- The New Testament is a compilation of 27 books written by approximately eight men.
- It is divided into four groups of books: five historical books, thirteen Pauline epistles, eight general epistles and a prophetic book, outlining end-time events.
- The five historical books are Matthew, Mark, Luke, John and Acts.
- Matthew, Mark, Luke and John are referred to as the Gospels, and they bear the names of their authors; Luke penned Acts.
- Nine of the thirteen Pauline epistles, which include Romans, 1st and 2nd Corinthians, Galatians, Ephesians, Philippians, Colossians and 1st and 2nd Thessalonians, were written to churches. First and 2nd Timothy and Titus were letters to pastors.
- Addressed to a wealthy slave owner, Philemon was a letter concerning forgiveness and restoration.
- The eight general epistles are Hebrews, James, 1st and 2nd Peter, 1st, 2nd and 3rd John and Jude.
- It is believed that Paul penned Hebrews, and the remaining general epistles bear the names of their authors.
- The prophetic book, which is Revelation, was authored by John.

This week's memory verse is Luke 1:49 (NT). Below, it is written.

**"For the Mighty One has done great things for me—holy is His name."**

**5.** Write this week's memory verse in the space provided. To assist you in learning it, repeat it to yourself several times.

_____

_____

# Lesson 2

# Matthew

In Lesson 1, you were presented with a brief overview of the books that comprise the New Testament. The first book, which bears the name of its author, is Matthew. Who was he? To find out, turn in your Bible to Matthew 9:9-13 (NT). Read this passage titled, "The Calling of Matthew." Answer the questions below by placing a check mark beside the correct answer.

**1.** Where was Matthew when Jesus called him?

   \_\_\_ a. at the synagogue
   \_\_\_ b. at a tax collector's booth
   \_\_\_ c. at his home

**2.** What did Matthew do when Jesus said, **"Follow me"**?

   \_\_\_ a. He refused to go.
   \_\_\_ b. He told Jesus he would go after he finished his work.
   \_\_\_ c. He got up and followed Jesus.

**3.** At whose home did Jesus dine later that day?

   \_\_\_ a. Matthew's
   \_\_\_ b. another tax collector's
   \_\_\_ c. a Pharisee's

**4.** Who else joined them for dinner that night? (Check all that are correct.)

   \_\_\_ a. many tax collectors
   \_\_\_ b. sinners
   \_\_\_ c. other disciples

**5.** When the Pharisees saw this, what question did they ask Jesus' disciples?

      ____   a.    "Why does your teacher eat so much?"
      ____   b.    "Why doesn't your teacher eat with us?"
      ____   c.    "Why does your teacher eat with tax collectors and sinners?"

**6.** To whom did Jesus say He had come?

      ____   a.    sick people, sinners
      ____   b.    doctors
      ____   c.    healthy people

**7.** Finish this statement Jesus made in response to the Pharisees: "I desire _____, not _____" (verse 13).

      ____   a.    sacrifice, mercy
      ____   b.    mercy, sacrifice
      ____   c.    righteousness, sin

Israel was under Roman authority. In spite of that authority, there arose within the Jewish community powerful religious groups known as the Scribes, Pharisees and Sadducees. The Scribes and Pharisees were experts in the Law, which God had handed down to His people through Moses. Adding additional requirements to God's commands, the religious leaders made it impossible to obey God's Law. The Sadducees ruled the temple, including the Sanhedrin, which was the Jewish court system. The Jewish religious leaders of Jesus' day were more interested in legalism and politics than in God.

Although these religious groups had their differences, they shared a common hope. Waiting for a Deliverer to come and set them free from Roman authority, they knew that He would be a descendent of King David. Also, they believed that He would rule from David's throne in Jerusalem. Possessing the Old Testament scrolls, they knew the Law like the back of their hands. When God's Deliverer, Jesus, arrived on earth, however, He was neither received nor embraced by them. Since they were so self-righteous, they could not fathom that He would associate with sinners and tax collectors.

While dining at Matthew, the tax collector's house, Jesus responded to the Pharisees' accusations by saying, **"But go and learn what this means: 'I desire mercy, not sacrifice'"** (verse 13). Consumed with ceremonial rituals and animal sacrifices, the religious leaders had repeatedly overlooked the importance of love, forgiveness and mercy. Not only did Jesus preach these virtues, but He also practiced them as evidenced by His association with sinners and tax collectors. Imagine Matthew's awe that day as he witnessed Jesus' rebuttal to the elite Jewish religious leaders. Undoubtedly, Matthew was paying close attention. Did he realize that the religious leaders would eventually crucify the One who had extended such mercy to him?

After Jesus' death, resurrection and return to heaven, the Christian Church was born. The Church desperately needed God's written Word to provide instruction for living. Through the guidance of the Holy Spirit, the New Testament began to be written. Opening with the book of Matthew, the New Testament has served to guide Christians for many years in their journey with God.

It is believed that Matthew penned his Gospel to the Jews. He, himself, was of Jewish descent. Throughout the book of Matthew, there are countless references to how Jesus fulfilled Old Testament prophecies concerning the coming Messiah. Proving to the Jews that Jesus was, in fact, the Messiah about whom the prophets had spoken in the Old Testament was important to Matthew. Also in his book, Matthew covered Jesus' birth, His ministries in Galilee and Judea, His death, resurrection and final instructions to His disciples—**"Go and make disciples of all nations…"** (Matthew 28:19). Who better to write the first Gospel than a Jewish sinner turned disciple? After Jesus called him to follow, Matthew became one of the twelve disciples whom Jesus personally taught.

Matthew's story is a wonderful example of how God can transform a sinner into the likeness of Jesus if that person allows Him to do so. Through his choices, Matthew demonstrated the importance of dedicating your life to God in service to Him. After his conversion, Matthew followed Jesus for three years. After Jesus' ascension back to the Father, Matthew became an apostle. He continued to preach about the love and mercy of the One who saved a sinful tax collector and changed his life forever. Eventually, Matthew was martyred because of his faith in Christ. Over 2,000 years later, Matthew's testimony is still changing lives today!

That's enough for today. Let's review what you have learned:

- When Jesus came to earth, Rome ruled Israel.
- Within the Jewish community, there arose powerful religious leaders known as Scribes, Pharisees and Sadducees.
- Matthew was a tax collector when he was called to follow the Lord.
- Matthew became a disciple of Christ.
- Being a Jew, Matthew's goal in writing his Gospel was to prove to the Jews that Jesus was the Messiah.
- After Jesus' ascension, Matthew became an apostle.
- Matthew continued preaching until he was martyred because of his faith.

This week's memory verse is Luke 1:49 (NT). Below, it is written.

**"For the Mighty One has done great things for me—holy is His name."**

**8.** Write this week's memory verse in the space provided. To assist you in learning it, repeat it to yourself several times.

_____

_____

# Lesson 3

# Mark

Unlike Matthew, Mark was not a disciple. He was not fortunate enough to actually meet Jesus and sit under His teachings. Mark, whose full name was John Mark, was an apostle. Arriving on the scene after Jesus' return to heaven, John Mark failed miserably when he first began in the ministry. As you will learn in today's lesson, however, God did not give up on John Mark. In time, he became worthy of the Lord's calling.

John Mark's mother was Jewish. His father was Roman. They resided in Jerusalem. John Mark's cousin was a man named Barnabas, who was a godly man full of compassion.

Preaching the Gospel, Barnabas and Paul traveled together. Devoting his life to serving God, Paul penned the majority of the New Testament. He will be examined in later lessons. On their first missionary journey, Paul and Barnabas were accompanied by John Mark. During the trip, John Mark decided for some unknown reason that he did not want to be there. Deserting them, he returned home to Jerusalem. This greatly upset Paul.

Sometime later, Paul and Barnabas were preparing for another missionary journey. Compassionately, Barnabas longed to give John Mark a second chance and invite him to go with them. Paul disagreed. Picking up with the story in Acts 15:36-41 (NT), read this passage titled, "Disagreement Between Paul and Barnabas."

Below are several statements taken from this passage. Put a "T" in front of those statements that are true. Put an "F" in front of those statements that are false.

____ **1.** Paul wanted to return to those towns where they had preached to see how the believers there were doing.

____ **2.** Paul suggested that he and Barnabas take John Mark with them.

_____ **3.** Paul did not think it was wise to take John Mark because he had deserted them in Pamphylia.

_____ **4.** Barnabas agreed with Paul that it would be better not to take John Mark along with them.

_____ **5.** Barnabas and Paul argued and decided to part ways.

_____ **6.** Barnabas took John Mark and went to Cyprus.

_____ **7.** Paul chose Silas to go with him.

What an unfortunate situation—a friendship torn apart because of anger. Sadly, this is an all-too-common occurrence between good friends. An argument takes place. Pride gets in the way, and neither person is big enough to apologize and forgive. So many friendships have ended because of pride. Tragically, the work that God had called Paul and Barnabas to accomplish as a team ended that day.

Although Barnabas was not heard from again, John Mark reappeared in the epistles, repeatedly commended by none other than Paul himself. Turning to the following verses, read both, which were penned by Paul.

Colossians 4:10 (NT)                    2$^{nd}$ Timothy 4:11 (NT)

**8.** In the space provided below, write your interpretation of Paul's opinion of John Mark according to these verses.

_____

_____

During his first imprisonment in Rome, Paul wrote to the church at Colosse. According to Paul's own admission, John Mark accompanied him. Additionally, Paul instructed the people to welcome John Mark should he come to visit them.

In 2$^{nd}$ Timothy 4:11, Paul wrote to Timothy again from a prison cell in Rome. He requested that Timothy bring John Mark along with him when he came to visit because Paul considered John Mark beneficial to his ministry.

Sadly, Paul's brother in Christ, Demas, had deserted him because of his love for the world. Apparently, Paul had changed his mind about John Mark.

The Gospel of Mark is a treasured account of Jesus' life, death and resurrection. Biblical scholars agree that Mark traveled with Peter, and that it was from Peter's firsthand experience as a disciple of Christ that Mark learned of the stories he penned. In his Gospel, Mark wrote about John the Baptist's ministry, Jesus' baptism and His temptation experience in the wilderness. John Mark also recorded information concerning Jesus' ministries both in Galilee and Judea. Mark's intended audience was Roman Gentiles who had converted first to Judaism and then later to Christianity. Portraying Jesus as Jehovah's Servant, John Mark provided ample illustrations of the Lord performing miracles and ministering to a hurting public.

From John Mark's example, we can learn that although we may fail, God is always willing to forgive us and give us another chance. That is exactly what He did for John Mark, and He will do it for you, too. Trust Him.

That's enough for today. Let's review what you've learned:

- John Mark's mother was Jewish, and his father, Roman.
- John Mark deserted Barnabas and Paul during a missionary tour.
- Barnabas and Paul split up because of a disagreement regarding John Mark.
- Traveling with Peter, John Mark grew to be a faithful apostle.
- Later, Paul found John Mark to be helpful to his ministry.
- Mark's intended audience was Roman Gentiles.
- In his Gospel, Mark portrayed Jesus as a Servant.

This week's memory verse is Luke 1:49 (NT). Below, it is written.

**"For the Mighty One has done great things for me—holy is His name."**

**9.** Write this week's memory verse in the space provided. To assist you in learning it, repeat it to yourself several times.

_____

_____

# Lesson 4

# Luke's Account of Mary and Elizabeth

Matthew, Mark and Luke are known as the Synoptic Gospels because they cover much of the same material. In Lesson 2, you discovered that Matthew, who was a Jew, was a tax collector before he became one of Jesus' disciples. Portraying Jesus as the Messiah, Matthew penned his Gospel to the Jews.

In Lesson 3, you were introduced to John Mark, who penned the book of Mark. Unlike Matthew, Mark was not a disciple. He traveled with Peter, who was one of Jesus' disciples. Mark's Gospel is an account of the information and events he learned from Peter. Mark wrote his book to the Romans and portrayed Jesus as a Servant.

Luke, who penned the books of Luke and Acts, also was not a disciple. Traveling with the apostle Paul, Luke's writings were an account of the events and information he learned in his travels. Luke was a physician. It is believed that he wrote to the Gentiles, and he emphasized the human side of Jesus.

Although each Gospel author wrote about Jesus, he may or may not have included particular events in his book. For example, only Luke recorded the coming births of John the Baptist and Jesus. Appearing first to John's father, Zechariah, the angel, Gabriel, later appeared to Jesus' mother, Mary, to announce the coming births of John and Jesus. After Mary received word that Elizabeth was expecting, and soon she would be, too, she paid Elizabeth a visit. Picking up with the story in Luke 1:39-56 (NT), read these passages titled, "Mary Visits Elizabeth," and "Mary's Song."

Answer the questions below by writing your answers in the spaces provided.

1.    When he heard Mary's voice, what did Elizabeth's baby do?

_____

_____

**2.** After greeting Mary, with whom did Elizabeth become filled?

_____

**3.** Why do you think Elizabeth said that Mary was blessed?

_____

**4.** In Mary's song, she praised God. List three statements that she made concerning Him.

_____

_____

_____

_____

_____

Why did God choose Elizabeth and Mary to mother two of the most important people ever born? For a clue, read Luke 1:5-6 and Luke 1:38 (NT). Answer the following question.

**5.** After reading these verses, why do you think God chose Mary and Elizabeth to mother Jesus and John the Baptist?

_____

_____

Looking about constantly for those on whom He can depend, God chose these two women because they served and obeyed Him. They were godly. Their names and their stories are known around the world because of their faithfulness and obedience to the Lord. God's desire is to carry out His will and His Word through His people. Are you preparing yourself in order that

God might choose you when the time is right? Reading and studying God's Word, as you are doing now, is an excellent way to prepare yourself for His calling. Stay in His Word so that when He calls upon you, you will be ready.

Throughout his book, Luke portrayed Jesus as a man. Certainly, the information contained within the pages of Luke related to the human side of Christ. There was much emphasis on Jesus' human dependence upon God through prayer.

Through parables such as The Good Samaritan and The Pharisee and the Publican, Luke emphasized relationships between people. Additionally, he recorded some of Jesus' miracles, which were not included elsewhere in the Bible, such as the Healing of the 10 Lepers. Interestingly, Luke penned more healing miracles than Matthew and Mark combined. Perhaps his position as a physician played a role in his emphasis upon miracles. Not only did he pen the book, which bears his name, but Luke also wrote the book of Acts.

In Lesson 5, you will revisit the book of Matthew to read about the Christ Child's miraculous escape from death. From the very beginning, the enemy was out to destroy our Lord. Because it was not yet time for Jesus to surrender His life, God warned Joseph of the enemy's evil scheme. It's an exciting adventure, and I'll see you there!

That's enough for today.  Let's review what you've learned:

- Matthew, Mark and Luke are known as the Synoptic Gospels.
- Luke was a physician who wrote to the Gentiles about Jesus, the man.
- Only Luke recorded the stories of the coming births of John the Baptist and Jesus.
- God chose Mary and Elizabeth because they served and obeyed Him.
- Preparing yourself now for God's call on your life is important.
- Exclusively found in the book of Luke are parables such as The Good Samaritan and The Pharisee and the Publican.
- Perhaps because he was a physician, Luke penned more healing miracles than Matthew and Mark combined.
- Additionally, Luke wrote the book of Acts.

This week's memory verse is Luke 1:49 (NT). Below, it is written.

**"For the Mighty One has done great things for me—holy is His name."**

**6.**  Write this week's memory verse in the space provided. To assist you in learning it, repeat it to yourself several times.

_____

_____

# It's time to take Test 1.

# Lesson 5

# Escaping to Egypt

In Lesson 4, you studied about the angel Garbriel's visit and announcement to Mary regarding the coming birth of Jesus. One might expect that the Son of God would make a grand entrance onto the earth. Surprisingly, that is not at all how He arrived. His life on earth began in a little town called Bethlehem. The Son of God was born in a stable rather than in a warm and inviting home. Humbly, He was placed in a manger, which was used to feed animals, instead of a baby bed. Unlike most newborn babies today, who are wrapped in a pink or blue cozy blanket, Jesus was wrapped in strips of cloth.

Under Roman authority at the time of Jesus' birth, the Jewish people were expecting a Deliverer but not at all in the manner that God chose to send Him. Although Jesus came just as the Old Testament prophets had described, Israel did not recognize Him. Expecting their Deliverer to be a mighty warrior, the Israelites believed He would free them from Roman authority. Establishing an earthly kingdom abundant with money and power was not Jesus' plan. Instead, He came to establish an eternal and spiritual kingdom and to restore mankind to a right relationship with God. Through His death and resurrection, He would enable God's Spirit to fall upon and inhabit all those who receive, believe and confess Jesus as Lord.

While most did not notice Jesus' arrival, there were others who did recognize His coming. Word spread that the King of the Jews had been born. Threatened by His birth, King Herod, who was the king of Rome at that time, summoned the wise men to question them regarding Christ's birth. Confirming that, indeed, the King had arrived, the wise men, or Magi, informed Herod that a star had appeared in the east at the time of Jesus' birth. Herod ordered the Magi to follow the star to Bethlehem and locate the Christ Child. Once they had identified Him, the Magi were to return to Herod to inform him of Jesus' whereabouts. Lying to the wise men, Herod said that he desired to find the Lord so that he could worship Him. His real motive was to destroy Jesus.

Picking up with the story, turn to Matthew 2:9-23 (NT). Read these verses. Below are incomplete sentences related to this passage. Choose a word from the word list, and complete the sentences by writing your answers in the spaces provided.

**Word List**

| myrrh | Magi | Egypt | dream | Archelaus |
|-------|------|-------|-------|-----------|
| star | angel | ordered | death | Jeremiah |

1. Stopping directly over the place where Jesus was, the _____ led the wise men to Jesus.

2. Upon entering the house, the _____ bowed down and worshipped Jesus.

3. The Magi presented Jesus with gifts of gold, incense and _____.

4. Because the wise men were warned in a _____ not to return to Herod, they returned to their country by another route.

5. An _____ appeared to Joseph in a dream and commanded him to take Jesus and Mary to Egypt because Herod desired to kill Christ.

6. Joseph and his family remained in _____ until Herod's death.

7. Infuriated because he had been tricked, Herod _____ that all boys two years old and under residing in Bethlehem and its vicinity be killed.

8. Herod's horrific order confirmed what the prophet _____ had penned in the Old Testament.

9. After Herod's _____, an angel instructed Joseph to take his family and return to Israel.

**10.** Warned again in a dream that Herod's son, _____, was ruling over Judea, Joseph withdrew to a town called Nazareth.

Although Jesus was born in a stable, verse 11 states that the Magi located Him and His parents in a house. By the time the Magi found Jesus, He was a toddler rather than an infant. In fact, verse 11 identifies Him as a child. Additionally, Herod ordered that all boys two years old and under in and near Bethlehem be killed because the Magi had identified Jesus' birth date as occurring within the previous two years.

From the beginning, it was, indeed, the enemy's plan to destroy our Savior. Jesus' mission had not yet been fulfilled so Satan's plan to destroy the Christ Child was thwarted. God sent His angel to warn Joseph of Herod's plans. Led by the Spirit, Jesus' earthy father protected Him from harm. Little did the enemy know that by destroying Jesus, he would actually be cooperating with God in reconciling man to Himself. Once that debt had been paid in full, the door would open, enabling God's Spirit to inhabit man's flesh. With the Spirit of God living on the inside of him, man could finally win the raging battle over sin. Even in the midst of evil, God is always working!

That's enough for today. Let's review what you've learned:

- At the time of Jesus' birth, Rome ruled Israel.
- Jesus came to establish an eternal and spiritual kingdom.
- Upon Jesus' birth, word spread that the King of the Jews had been born.
- Threatened by the news of Jesus' birth, King Herod sent Magi to locate the Christ Child.
- An angel warned Joseph to take Jesus and Mary and flee to Egypt.
- Warned in a dream, the Magi did not return to King Herod.
- Infuriated, Herod ordered that every baby boy two and under living in and near Bethlehem be killed.
- When it was safe, an angel instructed Joseph to return to Israel.
- Joseph and his family settled in Nazareth.

This week's memory verse is found in Luke 2:52 (NT). Below, it is written.

**"And Jesus grew in wisdom and stature, and in favor with God and men."**

**11.** Write this week's memory verse in the space provided. To assist you in learning it, repeat it to yourself several times.

_____

_____

_____

# Lesson 6

# Jesus, the Boy

In Lesson 5, you discovered that although Jesus was born in Bethlehem, His family eventually settled in Nazareth. Imagine His childhood. What was He like as a child? Did He have many friends? Did He participate in any sports? What were His hobbies? Arising in our minds are countless questions. Unfortunately, there is only one story of Jesus, the Boy, recorded in Scripture. It is found in Luke 2:41-52 (NT). Turning there, read the passage titled, "The Boy Jesus at the Temple." Answer the questions below by placing a check mark beside the correct answer.

1.   How old was Jesus when His parents went up to the Passover Feast in Jerusalem?

        ____   a.   10
        ____   b.   12
        ____   c.   14

2.   When Jesus' parents left to return home, what did He do?

        ____   a.   He stayed behind in Jerusalem.
        ____   b.   He went with them.
        ____   c.   He traveled home with relatives.

3.   After arriving back in Jerusalem, how many days did Jesus' parents look before finding Him?

        ____   a.   2 days
        ____   b.   3 days
        ____   c.   4 days

4.   Where did Jesus' parents find Him?

        ____   a.   at a nearby park
        ____   b.   in a courtyard, playing with some other children
        ____   c.   in the temple courts

**5.** What was Jesus doing in the temple courtyard? (Check all that are correct.)

      ____    a.      sitting among the teachers
      ____    b.      listening and asking questions
      ____    c.      amazing all who heard Him

**6.** Had Jesus' parents been worried about Him?

      ____    a.      yes
      ____    b.      no

**7.** What did Jesus say to His parents when they found Him? (Check all that are correct.)

      ____    a.      "I'm so glad you found me!"
      ____    b.      "Why were you searching for me?"
      ____    c.      "Didn't you know I had to be in my Father's house?"

**8.** In verse 51, what did Jesus do?

      ____    a.      He begged His parents to let Him stay in Jerusalem.
      ____    b.      He went back to Nazareth with them, and He obeyed them.
      ____    c.      He argued with His parents about returning to Nazareth.

**9.** What else does it say in verse 52 about Jesus? (Check all that are correct.)

      ____    a.      He grew in wisdom.
      ____    b.      He grew in stature.
      ____    c.      He grew in favor with God and men.

From reading this passage, several characteristics about Jesus can be seen. He desired to be at the temple. The temple was the house of God. Wisely, Jesus knew that there He could learn about His Father. He understood that there He could also fellowship with others who were seeking God, too. It was customary in those days for the religious teachers to read God's Word aloud in the temple. Jesus desired to hear and to study God's Word because

He wanted to grow closer to His Father. Like Jesus, you, too, must draw close to God through His Word, the Bible, being in the Father's house and associating with other believers.

Obeying His parents, Jesus returned with them to Nazareth, setting an example for you to follow. Learning to obey your parents during your childhood prepares you to obey God once you are out on your own. Obedience toward God is essential if you want to be in a right relationship with Him. Over and over again in Scripture, God commands His children to obey Him. Through obedience to the Father, you can partake in the covenant blessings that Jesus unselfishly purchased for you while upon the cross. These blessings include: victory over sin and death, eternal life with the Father and Son, the infilling of the Holy Spirit, provision for your daily needs, healing and much more. God's commandments are for your protection. Choose to be Christ-like, and obey them.

Jesus became wiser not only in the academic realm, but also, and most importantly, spiritually. Becoming more pleasing first to God, Jesus also grew in favor with men. Sometimes, pleasing God means going against what is popular. Obeying God rather than people is always the right choice to make. Certainly, Jesus obeyed God by coming to earth, setting a godly example in the way that He lived and teaching the very words of the Father. Frequently, however, He did oppose men in His teachings. You'll study more about this opposition in the lessons that follow.

That's enough for today.  Let's review what you've learned:

- Even as a child, Jesus desired to be in His Father's house.
- At the age of 12, He stayed behind at the temple in Jerusalem.
- After three days, His parents found Jesus in the temple courtyard.
- Jesus was sitting among the teachers, listening and asking questions, amazing all who heard Him.
- Jesus returned home to Nazareth with His parents.
- Obeying His parents, Jesus grew in wisdom and in strength.
- Jesus also became more and more pleasing to God and to men.
- From Jesus' example, learn to press into God through His Word and fellowship with other believers.
- Obedience is vital in your relationship with God.
- Like Jesus, you must become stronger spiritually.

This week's memory verse is found in Luke 2:52 (NT). Below, it is written.

**"And Jesus grew in wisdom and stature, and in favor with God and men."**

**10.**   Write this week's memory verse in the space provided. To assist you in learning it, repeat it to yourself several times.

_____

_____

_____

# Lesson 7

# John the Baptist

In Lesson 4, you were introduced to Elizabeth, who was the mother of John the Baptist. Preaching in the desert, John the Baptist was a messenger of God. Faithfully, he urged others to repent of their sins in obedience to the Lord. Humbly, John devoted his life to God. Caring very little about the things most people value, John wore tattered clothes made of camel's hair. He ate locusts and wild honey.

Although John did not seek popularity among men, many sought him out in order to repent of their sins. Flocking to him in the desert, people from Jerusalem, Judea and across the Jordan confessed their sins and were baptized. Because he was drawing such a crowd, the Jewish religious leaders became suspicious of John the Baptist. Who was this man? Could he be the Christ? Turning to John 1:19-28 (NT), read John's humble response to these inquiries from the passage titled, "John the Baptist Denies Being the Christ." Answer the questions below by writing your answers in the spaces provided.

1. The Jewish priests and Levites asked John if he was the _____ ,

   _____ or the _____ .

2. Regarding each of the three identities, John's response was _____ .

3. To identify himself, John quoted the prophet, _____ .

4. To whom is John the Baptist referring in verses 26-27? _____ .

Denying that he was the Christ, Elijah or the Prophet, John the Baptist not only informed the religious leaders that Jesus had arrived, but he also accused them of not knowing Him. The next day, John baptized Jesus. Baptizing Him proved to be a turning point for John the Baptist. From that moment on, he became less important in the eyes of the people while Jesus became more important. Was John the Baptist upset by that? No, he was not.

Preparing the people for Jesus' coming was his purpose in life. Dedicating himself to doing just that, he had served the Lord well.

Although Jesus had arrived, John did not quit preaching. Fearlessly, he warned a king that marrying his sister-in-law was a sin. What happened to John because of his boldness and dedication? To find out, turn to Matthew 14:1-12, which is titled, "John the Baptist Beheaded," and read this passage.

Following are several statements taken from the passage you just read. Put a "T" in front of those statements that are true. Put an "F" in front of those statements that are false.

_____ **5.** Herod thought that Jesus was a resurrected John the Baptist.

_____ **6.** Herod had arrested John the Baptist because John spoke out against Herod's marriage to his brother's wife, Herodias.

_____ **7.** Regardless of what the people thought, Herod planned to kill John the Baptist.

_____ **8.** Herod promised an oath to his wife, Herodias.

_____ **9.** In exchange for a birthday dance, Herod promised to behead John the Baptist.

_____ **10.** Distressed, the king decided not to honor the oath.

_____ **11.** After retrieving John's body, his disciples went directly to Jesus to inform Him about John's death.

John the Baptist gave his life because he refused to compromise his values. Naturally, when Jesus learned of John's death, He was saddened. Not only had the two become friends, but they were also related. Although Jesus tried to get away by Himself to mourn John's death, the crowd would not allow Him to do so. Moved by compassion, Jesus put His own needs aside, which was so prevalent to His nature, and ministered to over 5,000 people. Miraculously, He fed them. Additionally, He healed their diseases. Jesus' grief would have to be put on hold because there were many ailing and hungry sheep who desperately needed His care.

Truly, John's death was a difficult trial for Jesus to endure. However, He was no stranger to trials and tribulation. Prior to John's death, Jesus faced Satan, who would soon influence Jesus' own disciple, Judas, to betray Him. In Lesson 8, you'll accompany Jesus to the wilderness where He faced the devil and victoriously overcame his temptations. See you there!

That's enough for today. Let's review what you've learned:

- John the Baptist was a messenger in the desert who prepared the people for Jesus' coming.
- The Jewish religious leaders asked John if he was the Christ, Elijah or the Prophet, and he denied all three identities.
- John informed the religious leaders that Jesus was among them and yet they did not know Him.
- John the Baptist baptized Jesus.
- After Jesus was baptized, He became more important in the eyes of the people, and John the Baptist became less important.
- Herod beheaded John the Baptist because John spoke out against Herod's marriage to his sister-in-law.
- Saddened by John's death, Jesus tried to get away by Himself.
- The crowds followed Jesus, and because of His compassion toward them, He put His own needs aside and ministered to over 5,000 people.

This week's memory verse is found in Luke 2:52 (NT). Below, it is written.

**"And Jesus grew in wisdom and stature, and in favor with God and men."**

**12.**  Write this week's memory verse in the space provided. To assist you in learning it, repeat it to yourself several times.

_____

_____

_____

# Lesson 8

# Jesus Is Tempted by the Devil

In Lesson 7, you read about Jesus' baptism. After He was baptized, Jesus was led by the Spirit of God into the desert where He was tempted by the devil. In this lesson, you will study about Jesus' meeting with him there. Learning the valuable lesson of how to defeat the devil in your own life, you are certain to be blessed by today's revelation of God's Word.

Turning in your Bible to Luke 4:1-13 (NT), read this passage titled, "The Temptation of Jesus." Answer the questions below by placing a check mark beside the correct answer.

1.  How many days did the devil tempt Jesus?

    ____  a.  4 days
    ____  b.  14 days
    ____  c.  40 days

2.  What was the first temptation that the devil presented to Jesus?

    ____  a.  Jesus was hungry, and the devil tempted Him to turn a stone into bread.
    ____  b.  Jesus was tired, and the devil tempted Him to turn a stone into a pillow.
    ____  c.  The devil tempted Jesus to trust in him, and all would work out fine.

3.  What did Jesus say to the devil's first temptation?

    ____  a.  "It is written: 'Satan, get thee behind me.'"
    ____  b.  "It is written: 'Man does not live on bread alone.'"
    ____  c.  "It is written: 'It is unlawful for man to eat bread alone.'"

4. What was the devil's second temptation?

    ____ a. He promised to give Jesus authority and splendor over all the kingdoms of the world if Jesus would worship him.

    ____ b. He promised to make Jesus second in command if Jesus would praise him.

    ____ c. He promised to leave Jesus alone if He would worship him.

5. What did Jesus say to the devil's second temptation?

    ____ a. "It is written: 'Satan, get thee behind me.'"

    ____ b. "It is written: 'Worship the Lord your God and serve him only.'"

    ____ c. "It is written: 'Do not worship and serve other gods.'"

6. What was the devil's third and last temptation? (Check all that are correct.)

    ____ a. He dared Jesus to throw Himself off the highest point of the temple in Jerusalem.

    ____ b. He actually quoted Scripture, confirming that God's angels would care for Jesus.

    ____ c. He said that God's angels would lift Jesus up in their hands so that He would not strike His foot against a stone.

7. What was Jesus' response to the devil's third and last temptation?

    ____ a. "It says: 'Do not quote the Word of God.'"

    ____ b. "Scripture says, 'Leave Me, Satan.'"

    ____ c. "It says: 'Do not put the Lord your God to the test.'"

8. After Jesus quoted Scripture for the third time, what did the devil do?

    ____ a. He continued to tempt Jesus.

    ____ b. He left Jesus temporarily.

    ____ c. He continued to quote Scripture to Jesus.

Crucifying His flesh while building up His spirit man, Jesus had been fasting, or not eating, for 40 days. Knowing that Jesus was hungry, the devil tempted Him first with food, instructing Jesus to turn a stone into bread. Jesus refused. Offering to give Jesus the kingdoms of the world if only He would bow and worship him, Satan tempted Jesus a second time. Jesus refused. Lastly, the devil tempted Jesus by telling Him to throw Himself off the temple to prove that He was, indeed, the Son of God. Certainly, God would send His angels to save Jesus. Jesus refused.

Why was it so important to Satan that Jesus submit to his temptations? Cunningly, the devil knew that if he could entice Jesus to bow to him, he would achieve the very goal that had brought about his demise in the first place. As a cherub angel, whose name was Lucifer, Satan once guarded the throne of God. Guarding God's throne was not enough for Lucifer, though, because he desired to be as powerful as God. He desperately wanted to be worshipped. Lucifer was cast out of heaven and down to earth because of his pride. He became Satan. Now, Jesus, the Son of God, was on his turf. Once again, Satan attempted to gain authority over God by deceiving Jesus into submitting to him. Jesus refused.

Think about it for a moment. If you had been Jesus in the desert with the devil, wouldn't you have been tempted to demonstrate your power in order to prove him wrong? Wisely, Jesus knew that was not God's plan. Allowing God's Spirit to lead and direct Him, Jesus submitted His own will over to the Father, allowing Him to call all of the shots. In fact, Jesus replied to each of the devil's temptations with the words, **"It is written."** He quoted the most powerful words that He knew, the very words of God. What incredible self-control Jesus demonstrated in that desert. What a wonderful example He has set for you to follow.

**STOP FOR TODAY. FINISH LESSON NEXT TIME.**

There will be times in your life, perhaps there already have been, when you will be tempted to say or do something that you know is not God's will for your life. What will you do? How will you overcome the temptations that will certainly come your way? Speaking God's Word, as Jesus did in the desert, will strengthen you so that you can resist the devil every time. There is so much power in the Word of God.

Appropriately titled, "The Armor of God," Ephesians 6:10-20 (NT) instructs believers how to defeat Satan. Turning to this passage, read it. Answer the questions that follow.

**9.** Why is it important that you put on the full armor of God?

_____

**10.** If our struggle is not with flesh and blood (or people), with whom is it?

_____

_____

**11.** There are six pieces that comprise the full armor of God. List them.

_____

_____

_____

_____

_____

_____

**12.** Once you are standing firm and clothed in the full armor of God, what should you do according to verses 18-20?

_____

_____

According to this passage, our battle is not with flesh and blood (or people) it is with Satan and his rulers, authorities, powers and spiritual forces of evil. Fear not because God has made available His armor for your protection and victory, but you must put it on daily. Around your waist, place the belt of truth. In John 14:6a (NT), Jesus said, **"I am the way and the truth and the life."** Boldly, you can place the breastplate of righteousness over your chest because your faith in Christ and obedience to Him has made you righteous in God's eyes. Strapping the Gospel of peace around your feet will prevent you from being moved by fear so that you can stand firm against the enemy. Taking up the shield of faith will extinguish the flaming arrows that the devil throws your way. The helmet of salvation, which you received when you accepted Jesus as your Lord and Savior, will protect you.

Finally, verse 17 says to take up the sword of the Spirit, which is God's Word. Jesus used this very powerful sword to defeat Satan in the desert. If you remove the "s" in sword, you are left with "word." Use it to defeat the enemies in your life. Pray. Confess God's Word over difficult situations. It will change circumstances and people. Try it! Below is a list of promises from God's Word. Find one that you would like to claim. Look it up, and write it down. Confess it aloud daily. Continue to praise God, and watch the situation begin to change!

| Promise | Scripture |
|---|---|
| Healing | Psalm 103:2-3 (OT) |
| Forgiveness of sins | 1 John 1:9 (NT) |
| Peace | Isaiah 26:3 (OT) |
| Protection | Psalm 91:1 (OT) |
| Overcoming fear | Philippians 4:6 (NT) |
| God's love | John 3:16 (NT) |
| Power over the devil | James 4:7 (NT) |
| God's ability to change you | 2 Corinthians 5:17-18 (NT) |
| Strength and cheerfulness | Romans 15:5 (NT) |
| | Philippians 4:13 (NT) |
| Wisdom, knowledge, happiness | Ecclesiastes 2:26 (OT) |
| Answered prayer | Mark 11:24 (NT) |
| Joy | Romans 5:11 (NT) |
| Salvation for unsaved loved ones | Acts 11:14 (NT) |
| Rest in God | Psalm 62:1 (OT) |

_____

_____

_____

_____

That's enough for today.  Let's review what you've learned:

- After His baptism, Jesus was led into the desert where He was tempted by the devil for 40 days.
- Jesus overcame the devil with God's Word!
- After the devil left Jesus, angels ministered to Him.
- When trouble comes knocking, answer with the Word of God.
- Daily, put on the full armor of God, which is listed in Ephesians 6:10-20, to defeat the enemy.

This week's memory verse is found in Luke 2:52 (NT). Below, it is written.

**"And Jesus grew in wisdom and stature, and in favor with God and men."**

**13.** Write this week's memory verse in the space provided. To assist you in learning it, repeat it to yourself several times.

_____

_____

_____

## It's time to take Test 2.

# Lesson 9

# The Parable of the Sower

In Lesson 8, you studied about Jesus' encounter with Satan in the desert. Demonstrating the power of God's Word, Jesus defeated the devil by using Scripture. In today's lesson, you will study a parable that Jesus both taught and explained. Through this parable, Jesus further illustrated the importance of God's Word in one's life.

In the Old Testament, the prophet Isaiah penned that the Messiah would speak in parables, which are short stories that make a moral or religious point by comparing two unrelated issues. Throughout His ministry, Jesus did, indeed, speak in parables. By comparing spiritual truths to natural issues, Jesus explained to the common man much about God and His kingdom. For many, however, the parables that Jesus taught were not easily understood. Understanding them required much contemplation and further study on the part of the hearer. Sadly, only a few really sought to know Jesus and the meaning of His teachings. According to Scripture, their hearts were calloused. Because of this, they missed the Christ. Their lives were unfruitful.

One of the most widely quoted parables that Jesus presented was the Parable of the Sower. Turning to Matthew 13:1-9 and 18-23 (NT), read these two sections from the passage titled, The Parable of the Sower. Following are several statements related to these passages. Place a "T" in front of those statements that are true. Place an "F" in front of those statements that are false.

____ **1.** Rather than teaching on the shore, Jesus spoke this parable from a boat.

____ **2.** The first seed that the farmer sowed fell along the path, and birds ate it.

____ **3.** Falling on rocky places, the second seed sprang up quickly.

_____ **4.** The shallow soil and blistering sun caused the second seed to wither.

_____ **5.** The third batch of seed fell among thorns, which choked the plants.

_____ **6.** Falling on poor soil, the last portion of seed sown produced an unhealthy crop.

_____ **7.** Jesus explained that the first seed represented a person who heard the message but did not understand it, allowing the evil one to come and snatch away the seed.

_____ **8.** The seed that fell on the rocky ground represented a man who heard the message and received it for eternity.

_____ **9.** Unfortunately, trouble and persecution came to the man represented by the rocky ground, and he quickly fell away.

_____ **10.** The seed that fell among the thorns represented a man who heard the word but allowed life's worries and the deceitfulness of wealth to choke it out of his heart.

_____ **11.** The man who heard and understood the word was represented by the seed that fell on good ground.

_____ **12.** The man described in statement 11 produced a crop yielding double what he had sown.

Undoubtedly, Jesus used this parable to illustrate the importance of God's Word in one's life. Represented by the seed, the message was sown into four different types of grounds. Only one ground contained good soil. The grounds were actually symbolic of four different types of hearts. Because three hearts were not focused on God's Word, those individuals were un-fruitful. They included:

- Those who did not understand the Word;
- Those who were not grounded or rooted in the Word;

- Those who were focused on life's worries or the desire for wealth instead of God's Word.

When we think of God's Word, naturally, the Bible comes to mind. John, the fourth Gospel writer, penned that Jesus is the Word. The two are synonymous. Turn in your Bible to John 1:1-2 (NT). After you read these verses, skip down to verse 14, and read it too. Answer the question that follows by writing your answer in the space provided.

**13.** According to these verses, who is the Word? _____

Jesus is the Word. Although the Word was among men, they denied His identity. Today, Jesus is still among us in His Word yet many people do not recognize Him. Additionally, the Holy Spirit, who was sent on the Day of Pentecost, resides in the hearts of those who believe and confess Jesus as Lord. As we focus on Jesus, God's Word, His Spirit teaches and reveals truths to our hearts. We must make a choice, however, to seek Him with all of our being. Grounded in His Word, we must choose daily to be focused on Him rather than the pursuit of riches and the worries of this world. Only then will we produce a harvest that is far greater than what we have sown. What are you planting in your life? Hopefully, you are planting God's Word into your heart!

That's enough for today. Let's review what you've learned:

- Throughout His ministry, Jesus spoke in parables.
- In the Parable of the Sower, which Jesus explained, three unfruitful types of people were revealed: those who did not understand the Word, those who were not grounded in the Word, and those who were focused on riches and worries rather than on God's Word.
- According to John, Jesus is the Word.
- Spending time with Jesus and allowing the Holy Spirit to work within will enable you to produce a harvest far greater than what you have sown.
- Daily, plant God's Word, who is Jesus, into your heart.

This week's memory verse is found in Matthew 25:40 (NT). Below, it is printed.

**"The King will reply, 'I tell you the truth, whatever you did for one of the least of these brothers of mine, you did for me.'"**

**14.** Below, write this week's memory verse. To assist you in learning it, repeat it to yourself several times.

_____

_____

_____

# Lesson 10

# Jesus' Compassion for Others

During His ministry, Jesus identified the two most important commandments of God. Turning in your Bible to Matthew 22:37-39 (NT), read these verses to discover what He said.

1.  Write in the space below the two great commandments in these verses.

    _____

    _____

All of God's commandments are centered on loving Him and loving others. Not only did Jesus teach these commands, but He also lived them. Loving God so much, He agreed to temporarily surrender His position at the right hand of the Father in order that the world might be saved. This was the will of the Father, and Jesus submitted to that will.

Coming down to earth, Jesus not only proved His love and submission to God, but He also demonstrated His compassion for humanity. Changing water to wine at a wedding feast in Cana, healing the sick and resurrecting the dead were examples of His demonstration of compassion. Ultimately though more than any other act He performed, Jesus' suffering and death confirmed His love for mankind. The excruciating pain that Jesus endured in order that man could be reconciled to God proved His love for all people.

Throughout His ministry, Jesus performed the miracle of healing more than any other miracle. Why? Turning in your Bible to Psalm 145:8-9 (OT), read these verses to discover the answer to this question. Fill in the blanks that follow.

2.  "The Lord is gracious and _____, slow to anger

    and rich in _____. The Lord is good to all; he has

_____ on all he has made."

Out of His goodness, concern and love, Jesus came to earth to heal men and women. He came to teach them, and, most importantly, to save them. Why? He did so because of the great compassion He has for all of creation. He is so worthy of our praise.

One of the greatest examples of the compassion that Jesus possesses for others is found in Luke 7:11-17 (NT). Read this passage titled, "Jesus Raises a Widow's Son." Using the word list provided below, complete the sentences taken from this story.

# Word List

**news**      **prophet**   **widow's**   **Nain**   **God**   **heart**   **dead**

**3.**   Jesus was passing through a town called _____.

**4.**   A funeral was taking place for a _____ son.

**5.**   When Jesus saw the widow, His _____ went out to her.

**6.**   Jesus said, "'Young man, I say to you, get up!' The _____ man sat up and began to talk, and Jesus gave him back to his mother."

**7.**   The people were filled with awe and began to praise _____.

**8.**   The people called Jesus "a great _____."

**9.**   The _____ about Jesus spread throughout Judea and the surrounding country.

Jesus was under no obligation to stop and attend to the situation in Nain. He chose to because of His compassion. Jesus said to the grieving mother, **"Don't cry."** Quickly, the sadness that surrounded the funeral turned into joy. The people praised God! The miracles that Jesus performed led people to praise His Father. This is a significant indication that Jesus was God's Son because He glorified the Father rather than Himself. Glorifying God was Jesus' top priority. People were drawn to God because Jesus loved them and met their needs. Learn from His example. Love one another. Meet others' needs. As you do so, they will experience the love of God and draw near to Him.

That's enough for today. Let's review what you've learned:

- The two greatest commands that Jesus taught were: love the Lord God with all your heart, soul and mind; love others as you love yourself.
- More than any other miracle, Jesus performed the miracle of healing because He had compassion for those suffering.
- Jesus demonstrated God's love for others by raising the widow's son from the dead, thus drawing people to God.
- As you love others and meet their needs, they will be drawn to the Father.

This week's memory verse is found in Matthew 25:40 (NT). Below, it is printed.

**"The King will reply, 'I tell you the truth, whatever you did for one of the least of these brothers of mine, you did for me.'"**

**10.**   Write this week's memory verse in the space provided. To assist you in learning it, repeat it to yourself several times.

_____

_____

_____

# Lesson 11

# The Sheep and the Goats

During Jesus' ministry, He taught many different principles. Certainly, the most important one was love. God is love. He commands that His followers love Him and love others. As you will recall from Lesson 10, Jesus said that these are the two most important commandments of all. One day, Jesus will return to earth. When He does, He will be looking for those believers who are demonstrating love and kindness to others. One of His teachings on this subject is found in Matthew 25:31-46 (NT). After turning to this passage titled, "The Sheep and the Goats," read it. Answer the questions below by placing a check mark beside the correct answer.

1.   In this passage, who is coming back?

     \_\_\_\_   a.   God
     \_\_\_\_   b.   The Son of Man (Jesus)
     \_\_\_\_   c.   the nations

2.   When He returns, King Jesus will separate the nations into two groups: the sheep on the right and the goats on the left. To those on the right, what will the King say? (Check all that are correct.)

     \_\_\_\_   a.   "Come, you who are blessed by my Father."
     \_\_\_\_   b.   "Take your inheritance, the kingdom prepared for you since the creation of the world."
     \_\_\_\_   c.   "For I was hungry and you gave me something to eat."

3.   What else will the King say to those on His right? (Check all that are correct.)

     \_\_\_\_   a.   "I was thirsty and you gave me something to drink."
     \_\_\_\_   b.   "I was a stranger and you invited me in."
     \_\_\_\_   c.   "I needed clothes and you clothed me."
     \_\_\_\_   d.   "I was sick and you looked after me."
     \_\_\_\_   e.   "I was in prison and you came to visit me."

**4.** When the people on His right ask the King when they fed Him, gave Him a drink, invited Him in, gave Him clothes, took care of Him while He was sick and visited Him while He was in prison, what will be His reply?

_____ a. "Whatever you did for one of the least of these brothers of mine, you did for me."

_____ b. "Don't you remember all those times you did these things for me?"

_____ c. "I must have you confused with someone else."

**5.** What will the King say to those on His left? (Check all that are correct.)

_____ a. "Depart from me, you are cursed."

_____ b. "Depart… into the eternal fires prepared for the devil and his angels."

_____ c. "For I was hungry and you gave me nothing to eat."

**6.** What else will the King say to those on His left? (Check all that are correct.)

_____ a. "I was thirsty and you gave me nothing to drink."

_____ b. "I was a stranger and you did not invite me in."

_____ c. "I needed clothes and you did not clothe me."

_____ d. "I was sick and in prison and you did not look after me."

**7.** When those on the King's left say to Him, "Lord, when did we see you hungry or thirsty or a stranger or needing clothes or sick and in prison and did not help you?" what will be the King's reply?

_____ a. "Every time you did nothing for one of the least important of these, you did nothing unto me."

_____ b. "Whatever you did not do for one of the least of these, you did not do for me."

_____ c. "All of the time."

**8.**     According to the King, what will become of the people or the goats on His left?

    ____    a.    They will graze on grass the rest of their lives.
    ____    b.    They will be forgiven.
    ____    c.    They will go away to eternal punishment.

**9.**     According to the King, what will become of the people or the sheep on His right?

    ____    a.    They will receive eternal life.
    ____    b.    They will turn into goats.
    ____    c.    They will win a prize.

Jesus is the Son of Man or the King. Represented by the sheep are Christians who obey God's Word by loving and caring for others. Represented by the goats are those people who think that they are Christians, going to heaven, but are not allowed entry because they did not obey God's Word. Sadly, they did not love and care for those in need.

Jesus said that when you walk in love toward others, it is the same as doing it for Him. When you take care of the sick and those in prison, it is as if you are caring for Jesus. While it is true that believers are not saved by their works, Christians should be walking in the fruit of the Spirit if they are truly saved. The fruits of the spirit, which are described in Galatians 5:22-23, are love, joy, peace, patience, kindness, goodness, gentleness, faithfulness and self-control. Make a decision today to be kind and helpful to others. Your eternity depends on it. Additionally, you will experience a much more fulfilling life on earth if you obey God.

That's enough for today.  Let's review what you've learned:

- Jesus told the parable of "The Sheep and the Goats" to teach the importance of loving and caring for others.
- The sheep cared for others while the goats did not.
- Jesus rewarded the sheep with eternal life, but the goats were sent away to eternal punishment.
- As a believer, you have the responsibility to walk in love toward others.

- Jesus said that when you help others, it is the same as doing it for Him.

This week's memory verse is found in Matthew 25:40 (NT). Below, it is printed.

**"The King will reply, 'I tell you the truth, whatever you did for one of the least of these brothers of mine, you did for me.'"**

**10.** Below, write this week's memory verse. To assist you in learning it, repeat it to yourself several times.

_____

_____

_____

# Lesson 12

## The Importance of Humility

In Lessons 10 and 11, you discovered that Jesus carried the message of God's love to those whose lives He touched. Humility was also a virtue that Jesus not only taught, but He also demonstrated. In today's lesson, you will examine some of His teachings on this subject and witness an extremely humbling act that He performed. Hopefully, you will discover the value of such a virtue in your own life. Turning to Matthew 20:20-28 (NT), read this passage titled, "A Mother's Request." Below are several statements. Put a "T" in front of those statements that are true. Put an "F" in front of those statements that are false.

____  **1.**  The mother of Zebedee's sons asked Jesus for a favor.

____  **2.**  She asked Jesus to promise her that she would sit at His right or left hand in the kingdom.

____  **3.**  Jesus told the mother of Zebedee's sons that she did not know what she was asking.

____  **4.**  Jesus asked the two sons if they could drink from the cup of suffering from which He would drink.

____  **5.**  The sons of Zebedee said they could not drink from the cup of suffering.

____  **6.**  Jesus said it was up to Him who would sit where in Heaven.

____  **7.**  When the other disciples heard the favor that had been asked of Jesus, they became indignant (angry).

____  **8.**  According to Jesus, the disciples had to become like slaves if they wanted to become great or first in the kingdom.

___ **9.** Jesus instructed His disciples to pattern themselves after the Son of Man, serving rather than being served.

The sons of Zebedee were James and John. Pride had caused their mother to ask Jesus if they could sit at His right and left hand in the kingdom. Jesus declared that in order for them to be important or first, they must become servants just as He had come to serve man.

Let's turn now to a very humbling act that Jesus performed in order to demonstrate the importance of this virtue. Turning to John 13:1-17 (NT), read this passage titled, "Jesus Washes His Disciples' Feet." Below are several incomplete sentences taken from this passage. Using the word list provided, complete each sentence.

# Word List

| Jesus | disciples | feet | wash | example |
|-------|-----------|------|------|---------|
| loved | blessed | servant | Peter | devil |

**10.** Jesus washed His disciples' feet because He _____them.

**11.** The _____ had already prompted Judas Iscariot to betray Jesus.

**12.** Knowing what was in store for Him, _____ began washing the feet of His disciples.

**13.** At first, _____ did not want Jesus to wash his feet.

**14.** Jesus' reply to Peter was this, "Unless I _____ you, you have no part with me."

**15.** Peter then asked Jesus to wash not only his _____ but also his hands and head.

**16.** Jesus told His _____ that not all of them were clean.

**17.** Jesus washed the disciples' feet in order to set an _____ for them to follow.

**18.** Jesus told His disciples that a _____ is not more important than his master nor a messenger greater than the one who sent him.

**19.** According to Jesus, doers of the Word are _____.

Demonstrating humility was Jesus' purpose when He washed His disciples' feet. He commanded that they do as He did. Certainly, Jesus taught the importance of being a doer of His Word. Will you be a doer or a hearer only? Will you serve others? Make a decision today to follow Jesus' example.

That's enough for today. Let's review what you've learned:

- The mother of James and John asked Jesus if her sons could sit at His right and left hand in heaven.
- Replying to her request, Jesus taught the importance of serving.
- Jesus demonstrated the character trait of humility by washing the feet of His disciples.
- Jesus commanded those who follow Him to serve as He did.

This week's memory verse is found in Matthew 25:40 (NT). Below, it is printed.

**"The King will reply, 'I tell you the truth, whatever you did for one of the least of these brothers of mine, you did for me.'"**

**20.** Below, write this week's memory verse. To assist you in learning it, repeat it to yourself several times.

_____

_____

_____

# It's time to take Test 3.

# Lesson 13

## Arrested in Gethsemane

Over the last several lessons, you have studied about Jesus. Not only did He teach His followers to love God and others, but He also repeatedly demonstrated that love in His own life. John 15:13 (NT) says, **"Greater love has no one than this, that he lay down his life for his friends."** Unselfishly, Jesus laid down His life for all those who receive Him as Lord. In this lesson and the lessons that follow, you will discover what Jesus endured in order to restore mankind to God. He did it all for love.

Turning in your Bible to Mark 14:32-42 (NT), read this passage titled, "Gethsemane." Below are several statements. Put a "T" in front of those statements that are true. Put an "F" in front of those statements that are false.

____ 1. Jesus took no one with Him to pray in Gethsemane.

____ 2. Instructing His disciples to stay there and keep watch, Jesus prayed.

____ 3. Taking Peter, James and John along with Him, Jesus possessed a sense of peace regarding the circumstances that were about to unfold.

____ 4. Jesus desired that God's will be done rather than His own.

____ 5. The first time Jesus returned to His disciples, they were praying.

____ 6. Jesus told His disciples that the spirit is willing, but the body is weak.

____ 7. The second time Jesus returned, His disciples were sleeping.

____ 8. The third time Jesus returned, His disciples were praying.

____    **9.**    When Jesus returned for the third time, His betrayal was at hand.

Imagine for a moment what it must have been like for Jesus in the Garden of Gethsemane. According to Mark 14:33, He was deeply distressed and troubled. His purpose in coming to earth, which was to die for the sins of mankind, was about to unfold. Undoubtedly, Jesus knew that He would be beaten and mocked, tortured and killed. Scattering like sheep, His disciples would desert Him, and He knew it. Sadly, they could not even stay awake and pray for Him prior to His arrest. It would have been so easy for Jesus to back out and not go through with it all, and yet He surrendered His own will over to God.

Led by Judas Iscariot, the crowd sent by the high priest, chief priests, elders and teachers of the Law approached Jesus. What happened next? To find out, read Mark 14:43-52, which is titled, "Jesus Arrested." As you did before, mark the statements below with either a "T" or an "F."

____    **10.**    Those coming to arrest Jesus arrived unarmed.

____    **11.**    With a kiss, Judas betrayed Jesus.

____    **12.**    One of those present cut off Judas' ear.

____    **13.**    While Jesus questioned those opposing Him, He confirmed that His arrest fulfilled prophecy.

____    **14.**    Everyone deserted Jesus at the time of His arrest.

Jesus' disciples, who had witnessed His compassion, His miracles and His teachings, were now witnessing the fulfillment of Scripture in His arrest yet they deserted Him. Fear drove them away from their Savior. Greed provoked Judas into becoming a traitor for a measly 30 pieces of silver. Acknowledging Jesus' identity with a kiss, Judas led the crowd to the Lord. Provoked by jealousy and hate, the high priest, chief priests, elders and teachers of the Law had Jesus arrested. They were jealous of Him because He loved in a manner in which they could neither comprehend nor attain. He could perform the miraculous, and people were drawn to Him. Jesus spoke out against their self-righteousness and hypocrisy. Exposing the religious leaders in public, Jesus put them in their rightful place. This was more than they could bear so they seized Him in order that they might destroy the One who ironically came to save them.

In Lesson 14, you'll read about what occurred after Jesus' arrest in the Garden of Gethsemane. Tortured and mocked, stripped and beaten, the Son of God was crucified.

That's enough for today. Let's review what you've learned:

- In the Garden of Gethsemane, Jesus chose God's will over His own.
- His own disciples could not even stay awake and pray for Jesus.
- After He prayed, Jesus was betrayed by one of His own with a kiss.
- Upon Jesus' arrest, His disciples scattered like sheep.
- Jesus was taken to the Jewish religious leaders.

This week's memory verse is found in John 3:17 (NT). Below, it is printed.

**"For God did not send his Son into the world to condemn the world, but to save the world through him."**

**15.**   Write this week's memory verse in the space provided. To assist you in learning it, repeat it to yourself several times.

_____

_____

_____

_____

# Lesson 14

# The Savior's Death

In Lesson 13, you studied about the prayer that Jesus prayed in Gethsemane. During the hours that followed that prayer, Jesus faced treatment that was both barbaric and inhumane. In today's lesson, you will discover exactly what He endured as the Savior was led to Calvary and nailed to the cross.

Turning in your Bible to Luke 23:26-43 (NT), read this passage titled, "The Crucifixion." Answer the questions below by placing a check mark beside the correct answer.

1.  Who carried Jesus' cross after He became too weak to do so?

    ____ a.    Jesus
    ____ b.    Simon
    ____ c.    Cyrene

2.  As Jesus' mourners followed behind Him, what did He say to them? (Check all that are correct.)

    ____ a.    He instructed them not to weep for Him but rather for themselves and their children.
    ____ b.    He said they would one day consider the barren women blessed.
    ____ c.    He warned that in the future, they would beg the mountains to fall and the hills to cover them.

3.  How many other men were also led out with Jesus to be executed?

    ____ a.    three
    ____ b.    four
    ____ c.    two

**4.** While hanging on the cross, what did Jesus ask His Father God to do?

    \_\_\_\_    a.    forgive those who crucified Him

    \_\_\_\_    b.    save Him

    \_\_\_\_    c.    let Him die quickly

**5.** In verses 34-38, what did the soldiers and rulers do to Jesus? (Check all answers that are correct.)

    \_\_\_\_    a.    divided up His clothes by casting lots

    \_\_\_\_    b.    sneered at Him

    \_\_\_\_    c.    suggested that He save Himself

    \_\_\_\_    d.    gave Him wine vinegar to drink

    \_\_\_\_    e.    placed a sign above His head that read, "THIS IS THE KING OF THE JEWS"

**6.** In verse 39, what did one of the criminals do to Jesus? (Check all answers that are correct.)

    \_\_\_\_    a.    insulted Him

    \_\_\_\_    b.    asked for His forgiveness

    \_\_\_\_    c.    asked Him if He was the Christ

    \_\_\_\_    d.    asked Him to save Himself as well as them

**7.** In verse 40, the other criminal scolded the first. In verses 40-41, what did he say? (Check all answers that are correct.)

    \_\_\_\_    a.    "Don't you fear God since you are under the same sentence?

    \_\_\_\_    b.    "We are punished justly."

    \_\_\_\_    c.    "For we are getting what our deeds deserve."

    \_\_\_\_    d.    "But this man has done nothing wrong."

**8.** In verse 42, what did the second criminal say to Jesus?

    \_\_\_\_    a.    "Jesus, remember me when you come into your kingdom."

    \_\_\_\_    b.    "Jesus, do something to save us from dying."

    \_\_\_\_    c.    "Jesus, can't you save yourself?"

**9.** In verse 43, what did Jesus say to the second criminal?

    ____    a.    "I'm giving my life for the sins of the world."

    ____    b.    "I tell you the truth, today you will be with me in paradise."

    ____    c.    "Although I could save myself, I choose to give my life away."

At the beginning of this passage, Jesus instructed those who mourned for Him not to do so. Instead, He said they should mourn for themselves. Jesus was referring to a time period 40 years in the future when the Romans would conquer the Jewish people, crucifying many. Punishing Israel because they crucified Jesus, God would allow this to occur.

Referring back to verse 34, read it again. Lovingly, Jesus asked His Father to forgive those who mocked and sneered at Him, cast lots for His clothes and eventually killed Him. In the midst of His horrible suffering and death, Jesus chose to forgive, which is another example of His love toward man. Pouring out that love for both God and man, Jesus left His throne in heaven and came to earth, seeking not money or power as do men. He wanted only God's will. Doing good and sharing God's love with all those who would receive it, Jesus also demonstrated the virtue of humility as He humbly surrendered His life in order that mankind could be forgiven of their sins and restored to a right relationship with God.

Although Jesus died on that cross, His story does not end there. On the third day, He rose from the grave! In Lesson 15 you will study about His resurrection and read His instructions to His followers for the days that followed. See you there!

That's enough for today. Let's review what you have learned:

- Simon from Cyrene carried Jesus' cross to the place where Jesus was crucified.
- Suffering physical pain and death, Jesus proved His love for mankind at the cross.
- While on the cross, Jesus asked His Father to forgive those who crucified Him.

- Through His death, Jesus made provision for mankind to be restored to God.
- Jesus rose on the third day.
- Some 40 years later, the Romans conquered the Jews, crucifying many, fulfilling what Jesus had predicted.

This week's memory verse is found in John 3:17 (NT). Below, it is printed.

**"For God did not send his Son into the world to condemn the world, but to save the world through him."**

**10.** Write this week's memory verse in the space provided. To assist you in learning it, repeat it to yourself several times.

_____

_____

_____

_____

# Lesson 15

# The Lord Has Risen!

When we left off in Lesson 14, Jesus had just been crucified. He was taken from the cross and buried in a tomb. His followers were terribly sad. Although Jesus had assured them before His death that He would rise again, they really did not understand what He meant. On the first day of the week after His crucifixion, a wonderful and miraculous event occurred. Turning in your Bible to Matthew 28:1-10 (NT), read this passage titled, "The Resurrection." Answer the following questions.

1.  Name the two women who went to Jesus' tomb _____

    _____

2.  Upon arriving at the tomb, what did these women see? _____

    _____

    _____

    _____

3.  Other than the two women, who witnessed this event, and what hap-

    pened to them? _____

    _____

4.  What did the angel tell the women? _____

    _____

    _____

**5.** As the women set off to tell Jesus' disciples of His resurrection, who

appeared to them? _____

**6.** What name did Jesus use to refer to His disciples? _____

Imagine the joy on the women's faces when Jesus presented Himself alive to them! Verse 9 says that they clasped His feet. Picture that. Think about it. Answer the question that follows.

**7.** Why would you clasp someone's feet? _____

_____

Perhaps the two women, who were both named Mary, could not bear the thought of their Lord leaving them again. Worshipping Him, they held onto His feet because they desperately wanted Him to stay. Recognizing this, Jesus said, **"Do not be afraid. Go and tell my brothers to go to Galilee; there they will see me."** No longer did Jesus refer to His followers as disciples but rather as brothers. This confirmed that Jesus' death and resurrection made a provision to restore mankind back into the family of God.

In obedience to Jesus' command, the brothers gathered in Galilee in hopes of seeing their risen Lord. To their amazement and joy, He appeared to them there. For 40 days, Jesus remained on the earth. Many people witnessed His presence. During this time, Jesus spoke to His brothers, giving them instructions for the days ahead. Before Jesus left the earth to return to His rightful position in heaven, He gave them what is referred to as the Great Commission. Turning in your Bible to Mark 16:15-20 (NT), read these verses. As you are reading, keep in mind that these commands apply to Jesus' brothers and sisters today, including you. Answer the questions that follow.

**8.** Write the two commands Jesus gave in verse 15. _____

_____

_____

**9.** Jesus said that those who believed and were baptized would be what?

_____

**10.** In verses 17-18, Jesus spoke of miraculous signs that believers would accomplish. Write these signs in the space provided.

_____

_____

_____

_____

_____

Jesus instructed His followers to go into all the world and preach the good news. The good news is that Jesus came to earth and died on the cross to save mankind from sickness and disease, sin and spiritual death. Through His death, people can receive forgiveness of their sins and eternal life if only they believe, confess and obey Him. In His name, Jesus said that believers would drive out demons, speak in new languages, drink deadly poison and pick up snakes and be unharmed. Jesus was not suggesting that His followers should intentionally drink poison or pick up deadly snakes. He was, however, promising to protect them from harm. Miraculously, His power would flow through them so that they might do signs and wonders as He had done. Through miraculous signs and wonders, the unsaved would believe and receive Jesus as Lord and Savior.

You might think that God could not use a young person to do His work on the earth. That is not true. David was just a young boy when he fought and killed Goliath. Solomon, David's son, was a young boy when he became king over Israel. All it takes is faith. Faith is believing in some thing or some one even though you cannot see that thing or person. God's children are told repeatedly in His Word to live by faith. Faith is the opposite of fear. Faith works by love. In other words, faith and love go hand in hand. It is impossible to walk in either without practicing both.

Today, it is just as important to obey the Great Commission as it was over 2,000 years ago when Jesus first spoke it. Wherever you are, share the love of Jesus Christ with those around you. If you will study God's Word, believe, and do what it says, other people will believe in Jesus because of the miracles God works through you.

That's enough for today. Let's review what you've learned:

- On the first day of the week, Jesus rose from the grave!
- Appearing first to the two Marys, Jesus instructed the women to inform His "brothers" to meet Him in Galilee.
- Before Jesus left the earth, He gave His followers the Great Commission.
- The Great Commission still applies to believers today.
- You have God's power working in you and can fulfill God's plan for your life if you have faith.
- Faith and love work together and are the opposite of fear.

This week's memory verse is found in John 3:17 (NT). Below, it is printed.

**"For God did not send his Son into the world to condemn the world, but to save the world through him."**

**11.** Write this week's memory verse in the space provided. To assist you in learning it, repeat it to yourself several times.

_____

_____

_____

_____

# Lesson 16

# Peter and John

In Lesson 15, you learned that before He left the earth, Jesus instructed His brothers to preach God's Word throughout the earth. Promising that His power would work through them, Jesus confirmed that they would be able to perform miracles in His name. Additionally, He promised that God would send a Helper, who is the Holy Spirit, in His place. Leading and directing Jesus' followers, the Holy Spirit would enable them to fulfill the Great Commission.

Within just a few days after Jesus' return to heaven, God sent the Holy Spirit to 120 of Jesus' followers. This special event became known as the Day of Pentecost. Those present were filled with the Holy Spirit. Boldness to preach the Gospel of Jesus Christ to the world came upon them. Miraculously, they began to perform miracles just as Jesus had promised.

As the religious leaders had persecuted Jesus, so they also persecuted His disciples. These disciples were now called "apostles." During this time, many were added to their number. Warning the apostles, the religious leaders threatened them against preaching about Jesus. They refused to listen.

Two apostles who refused to be silent were Peter and John. While Jesus was on the earth, they had served as His disciples and were extremely close to Him. Now apostles, Peter and John were filled with the Holy Spirit and willing to risk everything in order to serve their Lord.

Turning in your Bible to Acts 3:1-10 (NT), read this passage titled, "Peter Heals the Crippled Beggar." Answer the questions that follow by placing a check mark beside the correct answer.

1.  At what time were Peter and John going to the temple? (Check all that are correct.)

     ____   a.     at the time of prayer
     ____   b.     at the time of fasting
     ____   c.     at 3:00

**2.** Who asked them for money as they entered the temple courtyard?

    \_\_\_\_ a.     another apostle
    \_\_\_\_ b.     a crippled beggar
    \_\_\_\_ c.     a Pharisee

**3.** What was Peter's reply to the beggar?  (Check all that are correct.)

    \_\_\_\_ a.     "Look at us!"
    \_\_\_\_ b.     "Silver or gold I do not have."
    \_\_\_\_ c.     "But what I have I give you."
    \_\_\_\_ d.     "In the name of Jesus Christ of Nazareth, walk."

**4.** What happened to the crippled beggar when Peter took his hand?

    \_\_\_\_ a.     He fell over.
    \_\_\_\_ b.     He began to cry.
    \_\_\_\_ c.     He jumped to his feet and began to walk.

**5.** What did the man that was healed do next?

    \_\_\_\_ a.     He went into the temple courts, praising God.
    \_\_\_\_ b.     He ran home to tell his family.
    \_\_\_\_ c.     He became an apostle.

**6.** As the people saw the man walking, jumping and praising God, how did they respond? (Check all that are correct.)

    \_\_\_\_ a.     They were amazed.
    \_\_\_\_ b.     They were filled with wonder.
    \_\_\_\_ c.     They went and informed the chief priests of the situation.

Because of the miracles they were performing, Peter and John drew large crowds. Following the apostles, the people were hungry to know more about Jesus and His power. Preaching to them about Christ, Peter and John spoke of His death and resurrection. They accused the religious leaders of killing Jesus. This infuriated the religious leaders. It was not long before Peter and John were arrested and brought before the Sanhedrin, which was the Jewish court system. Peter, who was as bold as a lion, began preaching to them too.

Skipping over to Acts 4:8-22 (NT), read these verses from the passage titled, "Peter and John Before the Sanhedrin." Answer the following questions.

7. According to Peter, who was responsible for healing the crippled beggar?

    ____   a.    Peter
    ____   b.    John
    ____   c.    Jesus

8. In verse 13, what two adjectives were used to describe Peter and John?

    ____   a.    schooled and ordinary
    ____   b.    unschooled and ordinary
    ____   c.    well-educated and extraordinary

9. Why could the Sanhedrin do nothing against Peter and John?

    ____   a.    because the man who had been healed was present with them
    ____   b.    because the man who had been healed would not press charges
    ____   c.    because the man who had been healed was not present with them

10. After conferring among themselves, what did the Sanhedrin say or do to Peter and John? (Check all that are correct.)

    ____   a.    They commanded them not to speak about Jesus.
    ____   b.    They commanded them not to teach about Jesus.
    ____   c.    They commanded them to leave the area and never return.

11. Did Peter and John give the impression that they would obey the Sanhedrin's commands?

    ____   a.    yes
    ____   b.    no

**12.** Although the Sanhedrin threatened Peter and John, they could not decide how to punish them. Why?

    ____    a.    They could not agree on a suitable punishment.
    ____    b.    The people were praising God because of the miracle they had performed.
    ____    c.    Peter and John left before they could punish them.

Although they were ordered to be quiet and not to speak or teach in Jesus' name, Peter and John refused. In the presence of the powerful Sanhedrin, the apostles boldly proclaimed that they would obey God rather than their commands. After they were released, they continued to preach God's Word even though it was very dangerous for them to do so.

Leaving behind some wonderful books in the Bible, Peter and John continue today to preach about Jesus. Peter wrote 1$^{st}$ and 2$^{nd}$ Peter. Both books were written to Christians suffering for the sake of Christ. Peter wrote to cheer them up and to encourage them to be brave. His books are still encouraging Christians today. John wrote the Gospel of John, which many believe to be one of the most beautiful books in the New Testament, as well as 1$^{st}$, 2$^{nd}$ and 3$^{rd}$ John. He also penned the book of Revelation which is a prophetic book concerning end-time events.

Thank God for courageous men like John and Peter who risked their lives in order that others might be saved. In Lesson 18, you will read about a man who lost his life because he refused to stop preaching about Jesus. First, however, you will study about a man and wife who were disloyal to God. What happened to them? You'll discover the answer to this question in Lesson 17. See you there!

That's enough for today. Let's review what you've learned:

- Peter and John were disciples who became apostles.
- Peter and John received the Holy Spirit.
- In Jesus' name, Peter and John performed miracles.
- Although they were warned to be quiet, Peter and John refused.
- They risked their lives so that others could be saved.

This week's memory verse is found in John 3:17 (NT). Below, it is printed.

**"For God did not send his Son into the world to condemn the world, but to save the world through him."**

**13.** Write this week's memory verse in the space provided. To assist you in learning it, repeat it to yourself several times.

_____

_____

_____

_____

**It's time for Test 4.**

# Lesson 17

# Ananias and Sapphira

In this lesson, you will study about a married couple, Ananias and Sapphira. They experienced the privilege of being a part of the first Christian church in the New Testament. Certainly, God had great plans for the two of them if only they had obeyed Him and humbled themselves. Instead, they chose to deceive God and let pride enter into their hearts. You will soon discover what became of them.

The church was growing. Everyone was helping one another. No one was in need of anything. Selling what they had, faithful Christians were giving the proceeds to the church. Ananias and Sapphira were no exception. After all, how would it look if they did not give? Selling a piece of their property, the couple said that they were giving all of the profit to the church. Were they really?

Turning in your Bible to Acts 5:1-11 (NT), read this passage titled, "Ananias and Sapphira." Answer the questions below by placing a check mark beside the correct answer.

1.  In verse 2, what had Ananias done? (Check all that are correct.)

    ____ a.   brought only part of the money from the sale of the land to the apostles
    ____ b.   kept part of the money from the sale of the land
    ____ c.   brought all of the money from the sale of the land to the apostles

2.  In verse 3, who, according to Peter, had filled Ananias' heart?

    ____ a.   God
    ____ b.   Sapphira
    ____ c.   Satan

**3.** After Peter told Ananias that he had lied to God, what happened?

    \_\_\_\_ a.    Ananias fell dead.
    \_\_\_\_ b.    Ananias asked for forgiveness.
    \_\_\_\_ c.    Ananias angrily stormed out of the room.

**4.** Three hours later, Sapphira came in. Did she lie to Peter about the money too?

    \_\_\_\_ a.    yes
    \_\_\_\_ b.    no

**5.** According to Peter, who had Sapphira tested (or lied to) about the money from the sale of the land?

    \_\_\_\_ a.    Peter
    \_\_\_\_ b.    Ananias
    \_\_\_\_ c.    the Spirit of the Lord

**6.** What happened to Sapphira?

    \_\_\_\_ a.    She asked for forgiveness.
    \_\_\_\_ b.    She died.
    \_\_\_\_ c.    She angrily stormed out of the room.

**7.** Ananias and his wife, Sapphira, made a foolish decision to lie about the amount of money they had made from the sale of their land. Why do you think they did so? Write your answer in the space provided.

_____

_____

_____

Perhaps Ananias and Sapphira wanted so desperately to look good in front of their fellow church members that they lied about the amount of money they were actually giving. Their sin was not in the amount they gave but in the lies they told. Confessing that their gift was the entire amount they had received from the sale of the land, Ananias and Sapphira lied to God. Not only did they lie to God, but they were also greedy. They kept part of the money for themselves. Obviously, they did not believe that God would take care of them if they were faithful tithers.

Definitely, Ananias and Sapphira were filled with pride. Did you notice that Peter told Ananias that Satan had filled his heart? Satan, who was once a beautiful cherub angel named Lucifer, was full of pride. He wanted to be like God. That pride caused his fall from an angel to the devil. If Satan was filled with pride, and Ananias was filled with Satan, then Ananias, too, was filled with pride.

One of the characteristics of someone who is proud is that he always desires to look good in front of others. He wants to be popular and run with the "in" crowd. Certainly, that was the case with Ananias and Sapphira. They wanted to be considered among the wealthiest in the church.

Lying, greediness and pride are all sin. Sin is a serious matter with God as you learned from the passage you read today. Sadly, this is the only account of Ananias and Sapphira in the entire Bible. Why would God include their story in His Holy Word? He did so because He desires that we learn from their mistakes. Be honest with God. Be faithful to Him in every area, including the area of tithing. Run from lies, greediness and pride. All are destructive and potentially deadly! On the other hand, honesty, a giving heart and humility glorify God. Make a decision today to walk in these virtues rather than the behaviors displayed by Ananias and Sapphira.

That's enough for today. Let's review what you've learned:

- Ananias and Sapphira made a foolish decision to lie about the amount of money they had made from the sale of their land.
- They were greedy and prideful.
- Their sin cost Ananias and Sapphira their lives.
- Lies, greediness and pride are destructive.

This week's memory verse is Matthew 28:19-20a (NT). Below, it is written.

**"Therefore go and make disciples of all nations, baptizing them in the name of the Father and of the Son and of the Holy Spirit, and teaching them to obey everything I have commanded you."**

**8.**   Write this week's memory verse in the space provided. To assist you in learning it, repeat it to yourself several times.

_____

_____

_____

_____

_____

# Lesson 18

# Stephen

In Lesson 16, you studied about two men who refused to be quiet concerning Jesus although they were warned not to speak of Him. Filled with the Holy Spirit, Peter and John were as bold as lions. Persecuting those who were preaching Jesus as Lord, the religious leaders had many apostles arrested, beaten and thrown into jail.

Another man who refused to be quiet was Stephen. Stephen had not been a follower of the Lord for very long. According to the Bible, he was full of God's grace and power. He did great wonders and miracles. Infuriating the religious leaders, Stephen was arrested. The high priest questioned him. In response, Stephen boldly began preaching to the religious leaders.

The longer Stephen preached, the angrier the religious leaders became. Informing them that they had rejected and killed the Christ, Stephen was stepping on their toes in a big way. What happened next? To find out, turn to and read the passage titled, "The Stoning of Stephen," in Acts 7:54-60 (NT).

In the spaces provided, write your answers to the following questions taken from the passage you just read.

1.    When Stephen looked up toward heaven, what did he see?

_____

_____

2.    What did the religious leaders do to Stephen? _____

_____

3.    At whose feet were the clothes of those stoning Stephen laid? Was he

in agreement with Stephen's murder? _____

**4.** While he was being stoned, what did Stephen ask Jesus to do?

_____

_____

As Stephen preached to the religious leaders, they became greatly agitated at him. Why? Openly in front of these same religious leaders, Jesus had professed that He was the Son of Man. He also prophesied to them that He would one day be sitting at the right hand of the Father. To discover this for yourself, turn to Luke 22:66-71 (NT). Read these verses from the passage titled, "Jesus Before Pilate and Herod." Answer the following questions.

**5.** In this passage, who was questioning Jesus?  _____

_____

_____

_____

**6.** In verse 69, what title did Jesus use to refer to Himself?

_____

**7.** Jesus informed the council that in the future, He would be seated where?

_____

As Stephen preached, he began to profess the haunting words that Jesus had spoken concerning Himself to the Jewish religious leaders. Validating that Jesus was in fact the Son of God, Stephen went on to accuse the Jews of murdering their Lord. Infuriated, the Jewish religious leaders stoned him.

Stephen asked the Lord to forgive the people who were murdering him. While being crucified, Jesus asked the Father to forgive His murderers, too. How is it possible to have enough love in your heart to forgive someone for murder? It is possible because the Holy Spirit—God's own Spirit—lives inside of you. The Holy Spirit not only filled Stephen with power, but He also filled him with the love of God.

You will probably never have to forgive someone for murder. Undoubtedly, there will be countless opportunities over the course of your lifetime, however to forgive others for one offense or another. Will you follow Jesus' example? Will you choose to be like Stephen and forgive? If so, you will be eternally blessed for your obedience to God. Additionally, you will experience incredible peace during your lifetime on earth.

That's enough for today. Let' review what you've learned:

- Stephen was filled with the Spirit and did wonders and miracles.
- The religious leaders arrested Stephen.
- After he was arrested, Stephen began preaching to the religious leaders.
- Stephen confirmed the very words Jesus had spoken concerning Himself.
- Infuriated, the religious leaders began stoning Stephen.
- Saul was present at Stephen's murder and consented to it.
- While being stoned, Stephen asked the Lord to forgive those responsible for his death.

This week's memory verse is Matthew 28:19-20a (NT). Below, it is written.

**"Therefore go and make disciples of all nations, baptizing them in the name of the Father and of the Son and of the Holy Spirit, and teaching them to obey everything I have commanded you."**

**8.** Write this week's memory verse in the space provided. To assist you in learning it, repeat it to yourself several times.

_____

_____

_____

_____

_____

# Lesson 19

# Philip and the Ethiopian

After Stephen's death, which you studied about in Lesson 18, many of Jesus' followers left Jerusalem. Fearing they, too, would be killed, they traveled abroad, preaching Jesus to those whom they met. One such man who did so was named Philip. At one time, he sat under Jesus' discipleship. As an apostle, Philip was now preaching in Samaria. Performing signs and wonders in the name of Jesus, Philip drew large crowds as he professed to the people that Jesus was God's Son. Hearing of Philip's success in Samaria, other apostles such as Peter and John joined him there. After a time of great harvest in Samaria, Peter and John concluded that it was safe to return to Jerusalem. Philip remained in Samaria.

One day, an angel of the Lord instructed Philip to go south to a desert road that connected Jerusalem to Gaza. Philip obeyed. While traveling, Philip ran across a man who was journeying back from Jerusalem, where he worshipped. Picking up with the story, turn in your Bible to Acts 8:26-40 (NT). Read this passage titled, "Philip and the Ethiopian." Below are several statements taken from this passage. Put a "T" in front of those statements that are true. Put an "F" in front of those statements that are false.

_____ **1.** The Ethiopian man was in charge of the treasury of Candace, who was queen of the Ethiopians.

_____ **2.** When he met Philip, the Ethiopian man was reading from Isaiah.

_____ **3.** God's Spirit instructed the Ethiopian man to approach Philip.

_____ **4.** Philip asked the man if he understood what he was reading.

_____ **5.** The man told Philip that he understood what he was reading.

_____ **6.** From the book of Isaiah, the man was reading about Jesus.

_____ **7.** Philip explained to the man that Isaiah had penned the words about Jesus.

_____ **8.** Although the Ethiopian man listened to Philip, he did not believe and surrender to Christ.

_____ **9.** Philip stayed with the man for several days.

_____ **10.** Philip continued to preach about Jesus in other towns.

Searching the Scriptures, the Ethiopian man was hungry to learn more about God. As he was reading from the book of Isaiah, he came to a prophecy about Jesus. He did not understand about whom Isaiah was speaking. Up to that time, he had not heard of Jesus. Loving this man so much, God directed Philip right in his path so that he could tell him about Jesus. Once the man heard the Gospel, he immediately received it, and asked to be baptized. If only everyone who heard the good news of Jesus Christ could readily receive it like the Ethiopian man.

Once his work was done, Philip disappeared and was seen next at a place called Azotus. We read about him again in Acts 21:8 (NT). Paul, whom you will study about again in Lesson 20, mentioned that he stayed at Philip's house in Caesarea. Philip was still serving the Lord.

Nothing further is mentioned about the Ethiopian man. One fact is certain. After he met Philip on that road from Jerusalem to Gaza, he would never be the same again.

Every day God places people who need a touch from Him in your path. A kind word or a smile can turn another person's frown into a happy face.

Romans 10:14 (NT) says:

**"How, then, can they call on the one they have not believed in? And how can they believe in the one of whom they have not heard? And how can they hear without someone preaching to them?"**

God expects us to be like Philip, proclaiming the Gospel. Unless we tell others about God's love and what Jesus has done and will continue to do for them, they will not know about the Lord. God is still changing lives just as He changed the Ethiopian man's life that day. Will you allow Him to change someone's life through you?

That's enough for today. Let's review what you've learned:

- Philip was an apostle.
- Fearing for his life, Philip left Jerusalem and traveled to Samaria.
- On the road to Gaza, the angel of the Lord instructed Philip to travel down a specific path, leading him to an Ethiopian man who was seeking the Lord.
- God used Philip to teach the Ethiopian man about Jesus.
- Accepting Christ, the Ethiopian man was baptized.
- Philip continued to preach the good news.

This week's memory verse is Matthew 28:19-20a (NT). Below, it is written.

**"Therefore go and make disciples of all nations, baptizing them in the name of the Father and of the Son and of the Holy Spirit, and teaching them to obey everything I have commanded you."**

**11.** Write this week's memory verse in the space provided. To assist you in learning it, repeat it to yourself several times.

_____

_____

_____

_____

_____

# Lesson 20

# Saul Sees the Light

In lesson 18, you studied about the death of Stephen. During this time, Christians were greatly persecuted by Jews. One of the Jews who persecuted Christians was Saul. While Stephen was being stoned, Saul stood nearby, holding the coats of Stephen's murderers.

Deeply rooted in the Jewish religion, Saul received instruction from Gamaliel, who was a highly-respected Pharisee. A tentmaker by trade, Saul was a Roman citizen. After Stephen's death, Saul got a whim to go to a town named Damascus to arrest Christians there. However, God had something else in mind for Saul. On the road to Damascus, Jesus spoke to him. Amazingly, Saul was converted to Christianity! God changed his name to Paul. Unbelievably, this is the same Paul you studied about in the first few lessons of this workbook. He began preaching the very Way he had previously denied. Soon he found himself in trouble with the Jewish religious leaders.

As Paul was about to be taken captive for preaching the Gospel, he retold the story of what happened to him on the road to Damascus. Turning to Acts 22:1-21 (NT), read these verses from the passage titled, "Paul Speaks to the Crowd."

Below are several incomplete statements taken from the passage you just read. Using the word list below, complete each statement.

## Word List

| | | | |
|---|---|---|---|
| companions | eyes | light | prisoners |
| trance | Jesus | baptized | Ananias |
| Gentiles | law | Jerusalem | Saul | God |

1.    Saul was a Jew who was well trained in the _____ by Gamaliel.

2. Obtaining letters from the Jewish religious leaders, Saul set out for

   Damascus in order to take Christians as _____ back
   to Jerusalem.

3. As Saul was on the road to Damascus, a bright _____
   suddenly appeared to him.

4. When Saul asked who it was that was blinding and speaking to him,

   the voice said, "I am _____ of Nazareth, whom you are
   persecuting."

5. Jesus instructed _____ to go to Damascus, where he would
   be informed of his mission.

6. Saul's _____ led him because he was blind.

7. _____, who was a devout follower of Jesus, came to Saul.

8. Saul's _____ were opened.

9. Ananias informed Saul that _____ had chosen him to give witness
   to all people of what he had seen and heard—Jesus.

10. Immediately, Saul was _____, and his sins were washed
    away.

11. While in the temple, Saul fell into a _____, and Jesus
    spoke to him.

12. Jesus instructed Saul to leave _____because the people
    there would not accept his testimony about Jesus.

13. Jesus told Saul that He would send him to the _____.

The Jewish religious leaders had crucified Jesus. Preaching that He was the
resurrected Son of God was detested among the Jews. The last thing they

wanted was one of their own testifying that Jesus was the Son of God. Paul was proclaiming this very message. Facing possible imprisonment, Paul explained to the crowd that he had been wrong about Jesus. He described how Jesus had blinded him on his way to Damascus. From that moment on, Paul's life changed dramatically. After Paul's testimony, the crowd demanded that he be killed. Taking him into custody, the Roman officials prepared to beat Paul. Wisely, he informed them that he was a Roman citizen. Because it was illegal to proceed, the commander released Paul the following day to the custody of the chief priests and Sanhedrin, which was the Jewish court system.

Appealing to Ceasar, Paul was sent to Rome. In route, he survived being shipwrecked and bitten by a snake. Through it all, Paul utilized every opportunity to preach Jesus to those around him. As a result, many people came to know and accept Jesus as Lord. Eventually, Paul was released. It is believed that the entire ordeal lasted at least two years from start to finish. Paul used his time wisely in prison. During those two years, he penned Colossians, Philemon, Ephesians and Philippians.

Abandoning everything he knew in order that he might fulfill God's plan for his life, Paul wrote much of the New Testament. He suffered because of his zeal for Christ. His imprisonment in Rome was not the first time Paul had been arrested and taken into custody for preaching, and it wouldn't be his last. In Lesson 21, you will read about his imprisonment with a fellow apostle named Silas. You will discover that together they caused a jail-house rock! See you there!

That's enough for today.  Let's review what you've learned:

- On the way to Damascus to persecute Christians, Saul was blinded by the light of Jesus.
- Jesus asked Saul why he was persecuting Him.
- After he arrived in Damascus, Saul was visited by a man named Ananias, whom God had sent.
- Saul's sight was restored.
- Changing Saul's name to Paul, God commissioned Him to preach the Gospel to the Gentiles.

- Paul continually preached to the Jews and wound up in prison.
- During his prison time, Paul wrote several books in the New Testament.

This week's memory verse is Matthew 28:19-20a (NT). Below, it is written.

**"Therefore go and make disciples of all nations, baptizing them in the name of the Father and of the Son and of the Holy Spirit, and teaching them to obey everything I have commanded you."**

**14.** Write this week's memory verse in the space provided. To assist you in learning it, repeat it to yourself several times.

_____

_____

_____

_____

_____

**It's time to take Test 5.**

# Lesson 21

# Paul and Silas

In lesson 20, you studied about Paul. At one time, he had persecuted Christians. After his conversion, however, Paul willingly risked his life in order to preach the Gospel. During his ministry, Paul traveled on four major missionary journeys. Barnabas accompanied Paul on his first journey. Going back to Lesson 3, you will remember that Paul and Barnabas got into a disagreement concerning John Mark. This occurred just prior to Paul's second missionary journey. Rather than take Barnabas with him on this trip, Paul chose to take another fellow apostle named Silas.

Like Paul, Silas was also a fellow Roman citizen. While on their way to pray one afternoon, Paul and Silas were met by a woman who refused to stop following them. As she followed, she shouted at them. This continued for days. What did Paul and Silas do about it?  Picking up with the story in Acts 16:16-40 (NT), read these verses from the passage titled, "Paul and Silas in Prison." Answer the questions below by placing a check mark beside the correct answer.

**1.**   What did the woman who followed Paul and Silas do for a living?

    \_\_\_\_   a.    She was a fortune-teller.
    \_\_\_\_   b.    She presided over other fortune-tellers.
    \_\_\_\_   c.    She predicted the weather.

**2.**   Following Paul, what did the woman shout?

    \_\_\_\_   a.    "These men are not servants of the Most High God, who are telling you the way to be saved."
    \_\_\_\_   b.    "These men are servants of the Most High God, who are telling you the way to be saved."
    \_\_\_\_   c.    "These men are impostors."

**3.** After several days of this, what did Paul do?

    \_\_\_\_ a.    He asked the evil spirit to leave the woman in Jesus' name.

    \_\_\_\_ b.    He commanded the evil spirit to leave the woman in Jesus' name.

    \_\_\_\_ c.    He left the area.

**4.** When the owners of the woman realized what had happened, what did they do? (Check all that are correct.)

    \_\_\_\_ a.    They seized Paul and Silas.

    \_\_\_\_ b.    They dragged them into the marketplace.

    \_\_\_\_ c.    They brought them before the authorities.

**5.** Finding fault in Paul and Silas, what did the magistrates order to be done to them before they were thrown into jail? (Check all that are correct.)

    \_\_\_\_ a.    He ordered that they present their case before him.

    \_\_\_\_ b.    He ordered that they be stripped.

    \_\_\_\_ c.    He ordered that they be beaten.

**6.** The jailer was commanded to do what concerning Paul and Silas?

    \_\_\_\_ a.    carefully guard them

    \_\_\_\_ b.    allow them to walk freely around the prison

    \_\_\_\_ c.    place them in separate cells

**7.** About midnight, what did Paul and Silas begin to do? (Check all that are correct.)

    \_\_\_\_ a.    cry out to God

    \_\_\_\_ b.    pray to God

    \_\_\_\_ c.    sing hymns to the Lord

**8.** As the other prisoners listened, what happened in the prison?

       \_\_\_     a.       The guard forced Paul and Silas to be quiet.
       \_\_\_     b.       The other prisoners began to riot.
       \_\_\_     c.       An earthquake shook the prison.

**9.** When the jailer discovered that the cells had opened and the prisoners were freed, what did he decide to do?

       \_\_\_     a.       call for help
       \_\_\_     b.       kill himself
       \_\_\_     c.       kill the prisoners

**10.** Realizing that the prisoners were still there, how did the jailer respond to Paul's comments? (Check all that are correct.)

       \_\_\_     a.       Rushing into the prison, he called for the lights to be lit.
       \_\_\_     b.       Bringing Paul and Silas out, he fell trembling before them.
       \_\_\_     c.       He asked them how he could be saved.

**11.** After the jailer and his family were saved and baptized, what did he do for Paul and Silas? (Check all that are correct.)

       \_\_\_     a.       He washed their wounds.
       \_\_\_     b.       He brought them into his house.
       \_\_\_     c.       He set a meal before them.

**12.** Although Paul and Silas were released the next morning, why did they refuse to go quietly? (Check all that are correct.)

       \_\_\_     a.       They did not want to leave the jailer.
       \_\_\_     b.       They were Roman citizens and had been unfairly treated.
       \_\_\_     c.       They wanted to be officially escorted out of the prison.

**13.** Were Paul and Silas officially escorted out of the prison?

        ___   a.    yes
        ___   b.    no

Stripped and beaten, Paul and Silas were put in chains and thrown into jail because they cast an evil spirit out of a woman. Rather than crying and complaining to God, they began singing hymns and praying to the Father. Everyone in the prison could hear them. What a testimony of Paul and Silas' love toward and faith in God! In the midst of their praise, an earthquake hit the prison. It was a jailhouse rock! The doors flew open! Instead of running away, the two men stayed and shared the good news of Jesus Christ with the jailer. Unbelievably, the jailer and his entire family were saved! The next morning, Paul and Silas were released and officially escorted out of prison.

If you found yourself in Paul and Silas' position, would you be praising God? There is power in praise. Although trials come, believers are to praise and worship God regardless of their circumstances. When we do, miracles happen. Let Paul and Silas be an example to you. Learn from them to praise God in every situation. He loves you so much and is always there to help you.

That's enough for today. Let's review what you've learned:

- On their way to prayer, Paul and Silas encountered a woman who, for days, followed them, shouting.
- Paul cast the evil spirit out of the woman, preventing her from telling fortunes.
- The woman's masters had Paul and Silas arrested.
- After being beaten and thrown into prison, Paul and Silas praised God.
- As they praised God, an earthquake hit, and the prison doors flew open.
- Instead of running away, Paul and Silas stayed and shared the Gospel with the jailer.
- The jailer and his family were saved.
- The next morning, Paul and Silas were released from jail and received an official escort.

This week's memory verse is Acts 28:28 (NT). Below, it is written.

**"Therefore I want you to know that God's salvation has been sent to the Gentiles, and they will listen!"**

**14.** Write this week's memory verse in the space provided. To assist you in learning it, repeat it to yourself several times.

_____

_____

_____

# Lesson 22

# Peter's Vision

In Lessons 20 and 21, you studied about Paul. After his conversion, one of the first people Paul longed to meet was Peter. Undoubtedly, Paul had heard about the signs and wonders the Holy Spirit was performing through him. Perhaps Paul knew that Peter had been in Jesus' inner circle. Did he know that Peter had denied even knowing Jesus after His arrest? Regardless of his coward-like behavior prior to Jesus' death and resurrection, Peter was now a changed man.

While Paul was called to preach to Gentiles, Peter was called to preach to Jews. Considering Gentiles inferior to themselves, many Jews were prejudice toward them. Being prejudiced toward anyone is a sin. God decided to teach Peter and his fellow Jews a lesson.

About this time in Caesarea, a Gentile man, whose name was Cornelius, was diligently seeking God. While Cornelius was praying one day, God gave him a vision. In the vision, Cornelius was directed to send a delegation to Joppa to retrieve Peter. Immediately, Cornelius sent two men, who were household servants, to Joppa. As the two men set out toward Joppa, Peter had a vision. Turning in your Bible to Acts 10:9-16 (NT), read this passage titled, "Peter's Vision." Answer the questions below by writing your answers in the spaces provided.

1.     Describe what Peter saw in his vision.

    _____

    _____

    _____

    _____

**2.** What did the voice in Peter's vision say to him?

_____

**3.** Initially, did Peter obey the voice of the Lord? _____

**4.** How did the Lord respond to Peter's comment regarding eating unclean things?

_____

_____

**5.** How many times did the object in Peter's vision descend and ascend?

_____

Three times Peter witnessed this object like a great sheet descending from and ascending to heaven. On it appeared a variety of animals. Addressing Peter, the Lord commanded, **"Get up, Peter. Kill and eat."** Initially, Peter refused because to eat certain animals and birds was forbidden according to Jewish law. God did not relent. Before Peter, He continued to present the sheet, which contained unclean animals, reptiles and birds. Repeatedly, God commanded him to eat.

While Peter was attempting to discern the vision, the Holy Spirit spoke to Him, informing him that Cornelius' servants were arriving at his door at that very moment. The Spirit commanded Peter to accompany the men back to Cornelius' home. The next day, Peter, along with other apostles, went with the men to Caesarea.

In the meantime, Cornelius was getting ready for a crusade. Inviting all of his relatives to his home, he eagerly awaited Peter's arrival. As Peter entered his home, Cornelius bowed at his feet. Quickly, Peter reminded Cornelius that he was just a man and should not be worshipped. Suddenly, Peter understood the vision. Skipping down to verse 28, read it. Answer the question that follows.

**6.**      Write Peter's interpretation of the vision God had given him.

_____

_____

_____

_____

Through the vision, God had shown Peter that no man is inferior to another. Peter confirmed this in verses 34-35. Read these verses printed below.

**"Then Peter began to speak: 'I now realize how true it is that God does not show favoritism but accepts men from every nation who fear him and do what is right.'"**

Peter learned a valuable lesson that day. Through this account, readers can learn the same lesson—that God is not partial to anyone. He loves everyone equally regardless of race, color or nationality. He accepts all who fear and obey Him.

Peter began preaching to Cornelius and his household, telling them about Jesus' life, death and resurrection. What was the end result? To find out, read verses 44-48. Answer the question that follows.

**7.**      What further confirmation did God give to affirm His acceptance of Cornelius and his household?

_____

_____

_____

The Holy Spirit fell upon those Gentiles, amazing Peter and his fellow apostles! Immediately, Peter commanded that Cornelius and his family be baptized. Peter stayed a few more days in Caesarea. Certainly, there was much celebration among Cornelius' family and the apostles that day!

Quickly, word spread among the Jews that God's Spirit was falling upon the Gentiles. Peter was reprimanded for associating with the Gentiles. Explaining to his brethren all that had transpired, Peter convinced them that Christianity was not just for Jews! In the end, God was glorified because of His gift of repentance to all men.

That's enough for today. Let's review what you've learned:

- God called Peter to preach to the Jews.
- Cornelius was a Gentile who loved God.
- In a vision, God instructed Cornelius to send for Peter.
- In an effort to prove that He is not partial toward anyone, God gave Peter a vision.
- In Peter's vision, God instructed him to eat "unclean" food.
- Peter went to Cornelius' house and led him and his entire family to Christ.
- God poured out His Spirit on the Gentiles as well as the Jews.

This week's memory verse is Acts 28:28 (NT). Below, it is written.

**"Therefore I want you to know that God's salvation has been sent to the Gentiles, and they will listen!"**

**8.**    Write this week's memory verse in the space provided. Repeat it several times to yourself to assist you in learning it.

_____

_____

_____

# Lesson 23

# The Adventures of Paul

As you read the book of Acts, following Paul's missionary journeys, you will discover that he encountered one dangerous adventure after another. Meeting a variety of people along the way, Paul recorded his encounters with precise detail. Biblical scholars agree that Paul had a personal scribe who documented these facts. In this lesson, as well as Lesson 24, you will study about some of Paul's exciting adventures.

Regardless of where Paul traveled, he could not resist preaching to his Jewish brothers. Repeatedly, Paul would make the synagogue his first stop at every destination, preaching Jesus to all in attendance. Time and time again, Paul's persistence in reaching out to the Jews resulted in riots and turmoil. Frustrated with the Jews in a particular city where he had been preaching, Paul would shake the dust off his feet and vow to preach only to the Gentiles in that region. When circumstances got too risky, Paul moved on to the next town.

Leading him along the way, the Holy Spirit empowered Paul to perform incredible signs and wonders. People who witnessed God's power working through Paul were understandably amazed by it all. On Paul's third missionary journey, he encountered seven Jewish fellows in Ephesus who were so impressed with what they saw that they decided to try performing signs and wonders themselves. Although the result was definitely supernatural, it was not exactly what they were anticipating. Turning in your Bible to Acts 19:11-20 (NT), read these verses from the passage titled, "Paul in Ephesus." Answer the questions that follow by placing a check mark beside the correct answer.

1. What articles of Paul's clothing were powerful enough to heal the sick and drive out evil spirits? (Check all that are correct.)

    ____ a.    his handkerchiefs
    ____ b.    his aprons
    ____ c.    his scarf

**2.** Those who were trying to invoke the name of Jesus over people who were demon-possessed were of what religion?

    ____   a.    Christian
    ____   b.    Jewish
    ____   c.    neither a nor b

**3.** The seven sons of Sceva were really sons of whom?

    ____   a.    the devil
    ____   b.    a Jewish chief priest
    ____   c.    a prominent Gentile family in the town

**4.** When the evil spirit to whom the seven sons of Sceva were addressing spoke to them, what did he say? (Check all that are correct.)

    ____   a.    "Jesus I know."
    ____   b.    "I know about Paul."
    ____   c.    "But who are you?"

**5.** The man in which the evil spirit resided did what to the seven sons of Sceva? (Check all that are correct.)

    ____   a.    obeyed them
    ____   b.    beat them
    ____   c.    stripped them naked

**6.** When the residents of Ephesus discovered what had occurred, what was their reaction? (Check all that are correct.)

    ____   a.    They were seized with fear.
    ____   b.    They honored the name of Jesus.
    ____   c.    They publicly confessed their sins.

**7.** What did those who were practicing witchcraft do?

    ____   a.    cast a spell on Paul
    ____   b.    commanded Paul to leave Ephesus
    ____   c.    burned their sacred scrolls

Apparently, the seven sons of Sceva thought just anyone could exercise the gifts of healing. After all, they were sons of a Jewish chief priest. Certainly, they were "religious" enough. Obviously, they were not. The evil spirit, who resided in the possessed man, knew of Jesus. He knew of Paul. He realized that he had to submit to them because both possessed authority over him. The seven sons of Sceva, however, had no authority over the devil or any of his spirits because the Holy Spirit did not reside within them. To further illustrate this point, the sons were attacked, beaten and stripped. Fleeing for their lives, they ran away from the scene. News of what had transpired traveled throughout Ephesus. A revival took place! People were openly confessing their sins. Those practicing witchcraft burned their sacred scrolls. People were saved!

Shortly thereafter, a riot broke out in Ephesus, and Paul was forced to leave. Still on his third missionary journey, Paul traveled through Macedonia. From there, he went to Greece where he stayed for three months. Going back through Macedonia, Paul traveled on to Philippi and then to Troas, where he met with several fellow apostles. One evening, Paul preached well into the night because he was planning to leave the following day. While he was preaching, a tragic event occurred. To discover what it was, skip down to Acts 20:7-12 (NT). Read this passage titled, "Eutychus Raised from the Dead at Troas." Answer the questions that follow.

8.    Where were Paul and his companions meeting?

    ____    a.    in the basement of a building
    ____    b.    on the first story of a building
    ____    c.    in an upstairs room of a building

9.    Why did Eutychus fall? (Check all that are correct.)

    ____    a.    He was sitting on a window sill.
    ____    b.    He fell asleep.
    ____    c.    He was not paying attention.

**10.** When Paul picked up the dead young man, what did he do? (Check all that are correct.)

    _____    a.    He sobbed.
    _____    b.    He threw himself on him.
    _____    c.    He put his arms around him.

**11.** What happened to Eutychus?

    _____    a.    He died and went to heaven.
    _____    b.    He was taken to the emergency room.
    _____    c.    He was resurrected.

Through God's resurrecting power, Paul was able to bring Eutychus back to life. What a night! Imagine the reaction of those present who witnessed this mighty miracle. Undoubtedly, word of this incident spread, and, as a result, many people believed. Fortunately, the seven sons of Sceva didn't try to resurrect Eutychus. No telling what would have happened had they attempted such a feat.

As you can see, Paul's missionary journeys were filled with excitement and adventure. For each success Paul experienced, however, he also endured danger and suffering. In Lesson 24, you will conclude this workbook with a look at Paul's insistence to preach to his people, the Jews, in spite of the Holy Spirit's warnings not to do so. See you there!

That's enough for today. Let's review what you've learned:

- During his ministry, Paul completed four missionary journeys.
- While in Ephesus, Paul encountered the seven sons of Sceva.
- Trying to exercise the gifts of healing, the seven sons were beaten and stripped, fleeing for their lives.
- As a result, many practicing witchcraft in Ephesus were saved.
- While preaching on into the night, Paul's friend, Eutychus, fell from a third-story building and died.
- Through the power of God, Paul resurrected Eutychus.

This week's memory verse is Acts 28:28 (NT). Below, it is written.

**"Therefore I want you to know that God's salvation has been sent to the Gentiles, and they will listen!"**

**12.** Write this week's memory verse in the space provided. Repeat it several times to yourself to assist you in learning it.

_____

_____

_____

# Lesson 24

# A Final Look at Paul

Undeniably, Paul's conversion has had an incredible impact on the world of Christianity. During his lifetime, Paul made four missionary journeys. As he traveled from place to place, preaching Jesus, he planted churches. Wisely, Paul prepared the people there to take leadership roles in those churches. In his letters, which are known as the New Testament epistles, Paul offered much instruction regarding church issues. Today, churches continue to turn to Paul's epistles for guidance.

Of the 27 books that comprise the New Testament, Paul wrote 13. Possibly, he penned the book of Hebrews, too, which means that he wrote a total of 14 books. That is over half of the entire New Testament. Several of the books Paul wrote were penned while imprisoned in Rome. Paul was incarcerated twice there.

The Holy Spirit warned Paul that returning to Jerusalem would result in persecution, but Paul was determined to go back. He was arrested there between his third and fourth missionary journeys. That arrest led to his first Roman imprisonment. Although he was called to preach to the Gentiles, Paul continually ministered to the Jews, who were his own people. This cost him dearly. In today's lesson, you will examine two warnings given to Paul prior to his return to Jerusalem.

Paul knew that his days were numbered. It was as if he was choosing death over life by returning to Jerusalem. As he departed from Miletus, where he had summoned and met with the elders of the church at Ephesus, Paul tearfully informed them that they would most likely never see him again. Along with his companions, who are identified in Acts 20:4, Paul began making his way back to Jerusalem. Let's join him by turning to Acts 21 (NT). Read verses 1-6 from the passage titled, "On to Jerusalem."

Following are several statements related to this passage. Put a "T" in front of those statements that are true. Put an "F" in front of those statements that are false.

___ 1. After leaving the Ephesian elders, Paul's next stop was Cos.

___ 2. Paul remained in Cos for several days.

___ 3. From Cos, Paul traveled through Rhodes and Patara.

___ 4. Eventually, Paul and his companions landed at Tyre.

___ 5. After finding fellow disciples at Tyre, Paul stayed with them seven days.

___ 6. Through the Holy Spirit, the disciples urged Paul to return to Jerusalem.

___ 7. In spite of the warning given to Paul, he departed for Jerusalem.

___ 8. The disciples and their families refused to accompany Paul to the ship because he would not heed their warning.

Through the Spirit, the disciples at Tyre warned Paul not to return to Jerusalem. Why would Paul insist on going when he knew perfectly well what awaited him there? To discover the answer to this question, turn back to Acts 20:22-24 (NT).  Addressing the Ephesian elders, Paul was bidding them farewell. Read these verses. Answer the question below by writing your answer in the space provided.

9. Why would Paul go to Jerusalem knowing that prison and hardships awaited him there?

_____

_____

_____

_____

According to Paul himself, his life on earth meant nothing compared to the calling he had to testify to the Gospel of God's grace. What a testimony of Paul's dedication to Christ! Willing to die, Paul found true contentment in serving and obeying God.

The disciples in Tyre were not the only ones to warn Paul of what would befall him if he returned to Jerusalem. As he continued on his voyage, a prophet named Agabus warned Paul too. Picking up where you left off earlier, read Acts 21:7-16.

Following are several statements related to this passage. Put a "T" in front of those statements that are true. Put an "F" in front of those statements that are false.

_____ **10.** After leaving Tyre, Paul and his companions traveled to Ptolemais.

_____ **11.** Immediately after landing at Ptolemais, Paul departed for Caesarea.

_____ **12.** Staying at the house of Philip, Paul remained in Caesarea for a number of days.

_____ **13.** The prophet Agabus was from Judea.

_____ **14.** Taking Paul's belt, Agabus tied his own hands and feet with it.

_____ **15.** Through the Holy Spirit, Agabus warned Paul that he would be handed over to the Jews.

_____ **16.** Fellow believers who witnessed Agabus' prophecy, cried and begged Paul not to return to Jerusalem.

_____ **17.** Moved by their pleading, Paul decided to cancel his trip to Jerusalem.

_____ **18.** The people responded to Paul's decision by saying, "The Lord's will be done."

Again, in spite of fellow believers pleading with Paul not to go to Jerusalem, he insisted on going. In Acts 21:13, Paul said, **"Why are you weeping and breaking my heart? I am ready not only to be bound, but also to die in Jerusalem for the name of the Lord Jesus."** Paul did go to Jerusalem. There, he was arrested. In his defense, he preached Jesus to the Romans who arrested him. After discovering that Paul was a Roman citizen, they turned him over to his own, the Sanhedrin, the Jewish Court System. In front of the Sanhedrin, Paul, who at one time demonstrated allegiance to this elite Jewish group, preached Jesus. Infuriated by his message, the Jews plotted to kill Paul.

Miraculously, Paul was delivered into the hands of the Roman government and was transferred to Caesarea. Coming face-to-face with Felix, a Roman governor, Paul began preaching about righteousness, self-control and judgment. Fearfully, Felix ordered Paul to stop preaching. Not knowing exactly what to do with him, Felix imprisoned Paul for two years.

Felix was succeeded by Festus. Bringing up their charges before the new governor, the Jewish religious leaders were hoping to finally rid themselves of Paul once and for all. Finding himself before Festus and the Jews who were seeking to destroy him, Paul maintained his innocence. He appealed to Caesar.

Paul was sent to Rome in order that he might, as a Roman citizen, appeal. During his journey, Paul encountered a great storm and was shipwrecked on the island of Malta for three months. While on the island, Paul preached to the islanders. Surviving a deadly snakebite, Paul was invited to the home of the chief official of the island, where Paul healed the official's father. After this, others on the island who were sick came to Paul, and they were healed. When they were ready to sail for Rome, the islanders provided all the supplies they needed for the trip. Arriving in Rome, Paul was once again imprisoned. Acts concludes with Paul preaching under Roman guard while awaiting trial before Caesar. Eventually, Paul was released.

While his fourth missionary journey is not as easily traceable as his previous journeys, it is believed that Paul traveled to Spain, Crete, Miletus, Colosse, Ephesus, Philippi, Nicopolis, and back to Rome, where he was imprisoned for the last time. He was executed around 67 or 68 A.D. Certainly, he had come a long way from where he began on the road to Damascus. Like Jesus, Paul suffered great persecution because he refused to deny Jesus' Lordship.

Looking down upon the fruits of their labor, the two of them are most likely concluding that it was well worth the price they paid.

That's enough for today. Let's review what you've learned:

- After his third missionary journey, Paul insisted on returning to Jerusalem.
- The Holy Spirit warned Paul that hardships and prison awaited him there.
- The disciples in Tyre warned Paul not to return to Jerusalem.
- Agabus warned Paul not to return to Jerusalem.
- Willing to die for the cause of Christ, Paul set out for Jerusalem.
- At Jerusalem, Paul was arrested.
- Appealing to Caesar, Paul was sent to Rome.
- In route to Rome, Paul endured a storm and was shipwrecked.
- On the island of Malta, Paul preached and performed miracles of healing for a period of three months.
- The book of Acts concludes with Paul's arrival in Rome and his preaching before the Roman guard while imprisoned.
- Eventually, Paul was released and went on a fourth missionary journey.
- Paul ended up imprisoned in Rome again and was executed around 67-68 A.D.

This week's memory verse is Acts 28:28 (NT). Below, it is written.

**"Therefore I want you to know that God's salvation has been sent to the Gentiles, and they will listen!"**

**19.** Write this week's memory verse in the space provided. Repeat it several times to yourself to assist you in learning it.

_____

_____

_____

# It's time to take Test 6.

# NOTES

# Test 1

## Lessons 1-4

**Short Answer Questions.** Write your answers to the following questions in the spaces provided.

1.    List the first five books of the New Testament. _____, _____, _____, _____ and _____

2.    The thirteen books immediately following the first five in the New Testament are referred to as what? Why?

      _____

      _____

3.    How many books are included in the general epistles? _____

4.    Who do most biblical scholars credit with writing Hebrews? _____

5.    What is the last book in the New Testament, and who wrote it? _____,

      _____

**Multiple-choice Questions.** Put a check mark beside the correct answer in the following multiple-choice questions.

6.    When Jesus came to earth, what empire ruled Israel?

      ____    a.    Babylonian
      ____    b.    Roman
      ____    c.    Egyptian

7.    What trade did Matthew practice prior to meeting Jesus?

      ____    a.    tax collector
      ____    b.    tent maker
      ____    c.    fisherman

8.    In Matthew 9:9-13, what complaint did the Pharisees have against Jesus?

      ____    a.    He was ignoring the Pharisees.
      ____    b.    He was associating with sinners.
      ____    c.    He was not following the custom of washing before eating.

9.    In response to the Pharisees complaint, to whom did Jesus say He had come?

      ____    a.    religious people
      ____    b.    the sick, sinners
      ____    c.    healthy people

10. To what group of people did Matthew specifically write his Gospel?

    ____   a.    Jews
    ____   b.    Gentiles
    ____   c.    the entire world

**True/False Questions.** Following are several statements. Put a "T" in front of those statements that are true. Put an "F" in front of those statements that are false.

____ 11.    Mark, whose full name was John Mark, was one of Jesus' disciples.

____ 12.    Both of John Mark's parents were of Roman descent.

____ 13.    Paul and Barnabas parted ways because Barnabas wanted to take John Mark on a missionary journey with them, but Paul refused.

____ 14.    Mark portrayed Jesus as a servant.

____ 15.    Mark wrote his Gospel specifically to people of Jewish descent.

____ 16.    Luke was one of Jesus' disciples.

____ 17.    Only Luke recorded the stories of the coming births of Jesus and John the Baptist.

____ 18.    Luke's intended audience was Gentiles, and he portrayed Jesus as a man.

____ 19.    Perhaps because he was a physician, Luke penned more healing miracles than Matthew and Mark combined.

____ 20.    Mark is credited with writing the book of Acts.

21.    In the space provided below, write this week's memory verse and where it is located.

_____

_____

# Test 2

## Lessons 5-8

**Short Answer Questions.** Write your answers to the following questions in the spaces provided.

1.       Why was King Herod threatened by Jesus' birth? _____

_____

2.       For whom did Herod send in order to locate Jesus? _____

3.       To where did Joseph escape with Mary and Jesus? _____

4.       When Herod learned that those whom he had sent had returned to their own country instead of

reporting to him, what order did he decree? _____

_____

5.       Where did Joseph and his family finally settle? _____

**True/False Questions.** Below are several statements. Put a "T" in front of those statements that are true. Put an "F" in front of those statements that are false.

____       6.       Although He was born in Nazareth, Jesus grew up in Bethlehem.

____       7.       There are multiple stories of Jesus' boyhood in the Bible.

____       8.       When He accompanied His parents to the Passover Feast in Jerusalem, Jesus was 12 years old.

____       9.       Jesus stayed behind in Jerusalem while His parents unknowingly left without Him.

____       10.     Searching frantically for Jesus, Mary and Joseph discovered him in two days.

____       11.     John the Baptist preached each Sabbath at the temple or synagogue.

____       12.     The Jewish religious leaders asked John the Baptist if he was Christ, Elijah or the Prophet.

____       13.     Baptizing Jesus caused John the Baptist's popularity among men to soar.

____       14.     John the Baptist spoke out against Herod's marriage to his sister-in-law.

____       15.     After John the Baptist's death, Jesus spent several days by Himself, mourning John's death.

**Short Answer Questions.** Write your answers to the following questions in the spaces provided.

16-17.   After Jesus' baptism, where did the Spirit of God lead Him? Why?

_____

_____

18.   How many times did Satan tempt Jesus? _____

19.   What did Jesus use to defeat Satan? _____

20.   Who ministered to Jesus after His encounter with Satan? _____

21.   Below, write this week's memory verse and where it is found.

_____

_____

_____

# Test 3

## Lessons 9-12

**Short Answer Questions.** Write your answers to the following questions in the spaces provided.

1.  Write the title of the parable that Jesus both taught and explained. _____

2-4.  List the three types of people who, according to the parable in Question 1, would be unfruitful.

_____

_____

_____

5.  What Gospel writer wrote that Jesus is the Word? _____

**Multiple-choice Questions.** Put a check mark beside the correct answer in the following multiple-choice questions.

6.  According to Jesus, what are the two greatest commandments?

    ____ a.  loving God and loving others
    ____ b.  loving God and loving yourself
    ____ c.  loving others and loving yourself

7.  More than any other miracle, Jesus performed _____.

    ____ a.  the gifts of the Spirit
    ____ b.  the gifts of healing
    ____ c.  the gift of resurrection

8.  Check the adjectives below that describe God, according to Psalm 145:8-9.

    ____ a.  gracious
    ____ b.  compassionate
    ____ c.  good

9.  In Luke 7:11-17, whom did Jesus raise from the dead?

    ____ a.  Lazarus
    ____ b.  a widow's daughter
    ____ c.  a widow's son

10.  What did the people of Nain call Jesus?

    ____ a.  the Son of God
    ____ b.  a great prophet
    ____ c.  a great healer

**True/False Questions.** Below are several statements. Put a "T" in front of those statements that are true. Put an "F" in front of those statements that are false.

____ 11.  Perhaps the most important principle that Jesus taught was love.

____ 12.  "The Sheep and the Goats" was a story Jesus told in order to teach the importance of loving others.

____ 13.  In the story, "The Sheep and the Goats," the sheep were the ones who loved and cared for others while the goats did not.

____ 14.  According to Jesus, when you perform a kind deed toward someone else, it's the same as doing it for yourself.

____ 15.  Because of God's mercy, Christians who do not demonstrate God's love to others will still spend eternity with Him.

____ 16.  Peter and Andrew were the two disciples whose mother asked if they could sit at the right and left of Jesus in heaven.

____ 17.  To demonstrate the importance of humility, Jesus washed the feet of His disciples.

____ 18.  At first, John did not want Jesus to wash his feet.

____ 19.  Jesus told His disciples that all of them were clean.

____ 20.  Jesus commanded His followers to serve others rather than being served.

21.  Below, write this week's memory verse and where it is found.

_____

_____

_____

# Test 4

## Lessons 13-16

**Short Answer Questions.** Write your answers to the following questions in the spaces provided.

1-3. Who were the three disciples Jesus took with Him to pray at Gethsemane? _____,

_____ and _____

4. While Jesus was off by Himself praying at Gethsemane, how many times did He return to His

disciples and find them sleeping? _____

5. With what did Judas betray Jesus? _____

**Multiple-choice Questions.** Put a check mark beside the correct answer in the following multiple-choice questions.

6. Who carried Jesus' cross the rest of the way to Calvary?

   ___ a. Jesus
   ___ b. Simon
   ___ c. Cyrene

7. How many other men were crucified with Jesus?

   ___ a. two
   ___ b. three
   ___ c. four

8. Why did Jesus tell the mourners who were following Him to the cross not to weep for Him but rather for themselves?

   ___ a. He was referring to a time in the future when the Romans would attack and crucify many of the Jews.
   ___ b. He was referring to the fact that He would no longer be with them.
   ___ c. He was referring to the end times and the Tribulation.

9. While Jesus was on the cross, who asked that Jesus remember him?

   ___ a. one of Jesus' disciples
   ___ b. one of the soldiers present
   ___ c. one of the criminals who was being crucified along with Jesus

10. As He was being crucified, what did Jesus ask God to do?

   ___ a. allow Him to die quickly
   ___ b. punish justly those responsible for His death
   ___ c. forgive those responsible for His death

**True/False Questions.** Below are several statements. Put a "T" in front of those statements that are true. Put an "F" in front of those statements that are false.

_____  11.  Mary and Martha discovered that Jesus had risen from the grave.

_____  12.  On the stone, which had been rolled away from Jesus' tomb, an angel sat.

_____  13.  Guards who were present were so afraid, they ran from the place where Jesus had been buried.

_____  14.  Jesus appeared to the two women as they were on their way to inform Jesus' disciples of His resurrection.

_____  15.  Before He left to return to heaven, Jesus gave His followers certain commands known as the Great Commission.

_____  16.  Peter and John were disciples who became bold apostles.

_____  17.  Preaching and healing in Jesus' name, Peter and John were well liked among the Jewish religious leaders.

_____  18.  After healing a man, who had been crippled, Peter and John were arrested.

_____  19.  Before the Sanhedrin, which was the Jewish court system, Peter and John remained silent.

_____  20.  When threatened, Peter and John agreed not to preach about Jesus anymore.

21.  Write this week's memory verse and where it is found in the space provided below.

_____

_____

_____

_____

# Test 5

## Lessons 17-20

**Short Answer Questions.** Write your answers to the following questions in the spaces provided.

1-2.      What were the names of the husband and wife who lied to the Spirit of God? _____

_____

3.      According to Peter, who had filled their hearts? _____

4.      What happened to the husband and wife as a result of their sin? _____

5.      Why are lies, greediness and pride destructive? _____

_____

**Multiple-choice Questions.** Put a check mark beside the correct answer in the following questions.

6.      What was the name of the apostle who was arrested and later stoned?

      ____    a.    Saul
      ____    b.    Stephen
      ____    c.    Peter

7.      After he was arrested for preaching and performing signs and wonders in the name of Jesus, what did the apostle in Question 6 do?

      ____    a.    He began preaching to his accusers.
      ____    b.    He began praying for favor.
      ____    c.    He left town.

8.      What, in particular, infuriated the religious leaders about Stephen? (Check all that are correct.)

      ____    a.    When he looked up toward heaven, he said he saw the Son of Man standing at the right hand of the Father.
      ____    b.    To the religious leaders, Stephen repeated the exact words Jesus had spoken concerning Himself one day being at the right hand of God.
      ____    c.    Stephen accused Saul of persecuting Christians.

9.      Like Jesus, what did Stephen do while being stoned?

      ____    a.    He prayed that his murderers would be punished justly.
      ____    b.    He prayed that God's will be done.
      ____    c.    He asked God to forgive his murderers.

10.      At whose feet were the coats of Stephen's murderers laid while he was being stoned?

      ____    a.    Saul's
      ____    b.    the chief priests'
      ____    c.    the high priest's

**True/False Questions.** Below are several statements. Put a "T" in front of those statements that are true. Put an "F" in front of those statements that are false.

____    11.    An angel told Philip where to go in order to meet the Ethiopian man.

____    12.    The Ethiopian man was very poor.

____    13.    Reading from the book of Isaiah about Jesus, the Ethiopian man was confused when Philip met up with him.

____    14.    When Philip explained that Isaiah was referring to Jesus, the Son of God, the Ethiopian man asked to be baptized in Jesus' name.

____    15.    Philip disappeared right after he baptized the Ethiopian man.

____    16.    Saul was one of Jesus' disciples.

____    17.    Saul was a Jewish tentmaker who was highly trained in the law by Gamaliel.

____    18.    While on his way to Damascus to persecute Christians, Saul was blinded by the light of Jesus.

____    19.    After Saul's companions led him to Damascus, a man named Barnabas came to aid Saul in regaining his sight.

____    20.    Jesus instructed Saul that he would minister to Jews.

21.    Write this week's memory verse as well as where it is located in the space provided.

_____

_____

_____

_____

# Test 6

## Lessons 21-24

**Short Answer Questions.** Write your answers to the following questions in the spaces provided.

1-2. What were the names of the two apostles who were imprisoned because they cast an evil spirit out of a fortune-teller? _____

3. While in a jail cell, what were the two apostles referred to in Questions 1 and 2 doing at midnight?

   _____

4. What happened at the jail? _____

   _____

5. Who got saved that night? _____

**Multiple-choice Questions.** Put a check mark beside the correct answer in the following questions.

6. Who was the disciple turned apostle that had the vision about the sheet with the animals, reptiles and birds on it?

   ____ a. John
   ____ b. Paul
   ____ c. Peter

7. To whom was the apostle named in Question 6 called to preach?

   ____ a. Jews
   ____ b. Gentiles
   ____ c. Romans

8. Who was Cornelius? (Check all that are correct.)

   ____ a. a Gentile man
   ____ b. a Jewish man
   ____ c. a man who was diligently seeking God

9. What was the main point of the vision given to the apostle named in Question 6?

   ____ a. God shows favoritism.
   ____ b. God does not show favoritism.
   ____ c. You should only witness to those people to whom God specifically calls you to witness.

10. What further confirmation was given to prove that Gentiles as well as Jews could be saved? (Check all that are correct.)

    \_\_\_\_    a.    The Holy Spirit fell upon the Gentiles.
    \_\_\_\_    b.    They began speaking in tongues.
    \_\_\_\_    c.    They joined the local synagogue.

**True/False Questions.** Below are several statements. Put a "T" in front of those statements that are true. Put an "F" in front of those statements that are false.

\_\_\_\_    11.    During his ministry, Paul completed a total of three missionary journeys.

\_\_\_\_    12.    The seven sons of Sceva operated successfully in the gifts of healing.

\_\_\_\_    13.    Because of all that God accomplished through Paul at Ephesus, even those practicing witchcraft were saved.

\_\_\_\_    14.    Paul's friend, Eutychus, not only fell asleep during one of Paul's long sermons, but he also fell out of a third-story window and died.

\_\_\_\_    15.    Paul's visit to Troas was cut short due to Eutychus' death.

\_\_\_\_    16.    Through men like Agabus, the Holy Spirit warned Paul that returning to Jerusalem would be dangerous.

\_\_\_\_    17.    Paul heeded the warnings and changed his mind about going to Jerusalem.

\_\_\_\_    18.    After he was arrested in Jerusalem, Paul appealed to Caesar.

\_\_\_\_    19.    While imprisoned, Paul was unable to preach the Gospel of Christ.

\_\_\_\_    20.    Eventually, Paul was released and died of natural causes.

21.    Write this week's memory verse as well as where it is located in the space provided.

_____

_____

# Answer Key

## Lesson 1:

1. Matthew, Mark, Luke, John, Acts
2. Romans, 1st Corinthians, 2nd Corinthians, Galatians, Ephesians, Philippians, Colossians, 1st Thessalonians, 2nd Thessalonians, 1st Timothy, 2nd Timothy, Titus, Philemon
3. Hebrews, James, 1st Peter, 2nd Peter, 1st John, 2nd John, 3rd John, Jude
4. Revelation
5. "For the Mighty One has done great things for me—holy is His name" (Luke 1:49).

## Lesson 2:

1. b; 2.c; 3.a; 4.a,b,c; 5.c; 6.a; 7.b;
8. "For the Mighty One has done great things for me—holy is His name" (Luke 1:49).

## Lesson 3:

1. T; 2.F; 3.T; 4.F; 5.T; 6.T; 7.T;
8. Paul grew fond of John Mark and even found him beneficial to his ministry.
9. "For the Mighty One has done great things for me—holy is His name" (Luke 1:49).

## Lesson 4:

1. He leaped for joy inside her stomach.
2. She became filled with the Holy Spirit.
3. She was blessed to be Jesus' mother.
4. "He has been mindful of the humble state of his servant." "The Mighty One has done great things for me."
   "His mercy extends to those who fear him from generation to generation."
   "He has performed mighty deeds with his arm."
   "He has scattered those who are proud in their inmost thoughts."
   "He has brought down rulers from their thrones but has lifted up the humble."
   "He has filled the hungry with good things but has sent the rich away empty."
   "He has helped His servant Israel, remembering to be merciful to Abraham and his descendants forever, even as he said to our fathers."
5. They served and obeyed God.
6. "For the Mighty One has done great things for me—holy is His name" (Luke 1:49).

## Lesson 5:

1. star; 2.Magi; 3.myrrh; 4.dream; 5.angel; 6. Egypt; 7. ordered; 8.Jeremiah; 9.death; 10.Archelaus;
11. "And Jesus grew in wisdom and in stature, and in favor with God and men" (Luke 2:52).

## Lesson 6:

1. b; 2.a; 3.b; 4.c; 5.a,b,c; 6.a 7.b,c; 8.b; 9.a,b,c;
10. "And Jesus grew in wisdom and in stature, and in favor with God and men" (Luke 2:52).

Lesson 7:

1.        Christ, Elijah, Prophet; 2.no; 3.Isaiah; 4.Jesus; 5.T; 6.T; 7.F; 8.F; 9.T; 10.F; 11.T;
12.      "And Jesus grew in wisdom and in stature, and in favor with God and men" (Luke 2:52).

Lesson 8:

1.        c; 2.a; 3.b; 4.a; 5.b; 6.a,b,c; 7.c; 8.b;
9.        to defeat the enemy in your life
10.      It is with Satan, his rulers, authorities, powers and spiritual forces of evil.
11.      the belt of truth, breastplate of righteousness, Gospel of peace, shield of faith, helmet of salvation and sword of the Spirit
12.      pray. Pray also for fellow believers.
13.      "And Jesus grew in wisdom and in stature, and in favor with God and men" (Luke 2:52).

Lesson 9:

1.        T; 2.T; 3.T; 4.T; 5.T; 6.F; 7.T; 8.F; 9.T; 10.T; 11.T; 12.F; 13. Jesus
14.      "The King will reply, 'I tell you the truth, whatever you did for one of the least of these brothers of mine, you did for me'" Matthew 25:40 (NT).

Lesson 10:

1.        Love the Lord your God with all your heart, soul and mind.  Love your neighbor as yourself.
2.        compassionate, love, compassion
3.        Nain; 4.widow's; 5.heart; 6.dead; 7.God; 8.prophet; 9.news;
10.      "The King will reply, 'I tell you the truth, whatever you did for one of the least of these brothers of mine, you did for me'" Matthew 25:40 (NT).

Lesson 11:

1.        b; 2.a,b,c; 3.a,b,c,d,e; 4.a; 5.a,b,c; 6.a,b,c,d; 7.b; 8.c; 9.a;
10.      "The King will reply, 'I tell you the truth, whatever you did for one of the least of these brothers of mine, you did for me'" Matthew 25:40 (NT).

Lesson 12:

1.        T; 2.F; 3.T; 4.T; 5.F; 6.F; 7.T; 8.T; 9.T; 10.loved; 11.devil; 12.Jesus; 13.Peter; 14.wash; 15.feet;
16.      disciples; 17.example; 18.servant; 19.blessed;
20.      "The King will reply, 'I tell you the truth, whatever you did for one of the least of these brothers of mine, you did for me'" Matthew 25:40 (NT).

Lesson 13:

1.        F; 2.T; 3.F; 4.T; 5.F; 6.T; 7.T; 8.F; 9.T; 10.F; 11.T; 12.F; 13.T; 14.T;
15.      "For God did not send his Son into the world to condemn the world, but to save the world through him" (John 3:17).

Lesson 14:

1.        b; 2.a,b,c; 3.c; 4.a; 5.a,b,c,d,e,; 6.a,c,d; 7.a,b,c,d; 8.a; 9.b;
10.      "For God did not send his Son into the world to condemn the world, but to save the world through him" (John 3:17).

Lesson 15:

1. Mary and Mary Magdalene
2. They saw that the stone of Jesus' tomb had been rolled away. They also saw an angel sitting on the stone. His appearance was like lightning, and his clothes were as white as snow.
3. The guards. They were so afraid that they became like dead men.
4. Jesus had risen. Tell the disciples to meet Him in Galilee.
5. Jesus
6. Brothers
7. To prevent an individual from leaving you, you might clasp his/her feet.
8. Go into all the world. Preach the good news to all of creation.
9. Saved
10. They would drive out demons, speak in new tongues, pick up deadly snakes and drink poison without being harmed. They would heal the sick.
11. "For God did not send his Son into the world to condemn the world, but to save the world through him" (John 3:17).

Lesson 16:

1. a,c; 2.b; 3.a,b,c,d; 4.c; 5.a; 6.a,b; 7.c; 8.b; 9.a; 10.a,b; 11.b; 12.b;
13. "For God did not send his Son into the world to condemn the world, but to save the world through him" (John 3:17).

Lesson 17:

1. a,b; 2.c; 3.a; 4.a; 5.c; 6.b;
7. They were filled with greed and selfishness. They wanted to look good in front of others.
8. "Therefore go and make disciples of all nations, baptizing them in the name of the Father and of the Son and of the Holy Spirit and teaching them to obey everything I have commanded you" (Matthew 28:19-20a).

Lesson 18:

1. He saw the glory of God and Jesus standing on His right side.
2. They rushed at him, dragging him out of town and began stoning him.
3. Saul, yes
4. He asked Jesus to receive his spirit and forgive those responsible for his death.
5. the Jewish council of the elders and the people, the chief priests and teachers of the Law
6. the Son of Man
7. at the right hand of the mighty God
8. "Therefore go and make disciples of all nations, baptizing them in the name of the Father and of the Son and of the Holy Spirit and teaching them to obey everything I have commanded you" (Matthew 28:19-20a).

Lesson 19:

1. T; 2.T; 3.F; 4.T; 5.F; 6.T; 7.T; 8.F; 9.F; 10.T;
11. "Therefore go and make disciples of all nations, baptizing them in the name of the Father and of the Son and of the Holy Spirit and teaching them to obey everything I have commanded you" (Matthew 28:19-20a).

Lesson 20:

1. law; 2.prionsers; 3.light; 4.Jesus; 5.Saul; 6.companions; 7.Ananias; 8.eyes; 9.God; 10.baptized;
11. trance; 12.Jerusalem; 13.Gentiles;

14.　　 "Therefore go and make disciples of all nations, baptizing them in the name of the Father and of the Son and of the Holy Spirit and teaching them to obey everything I have commanded you" (Matthew 28:19-20a).

Lesson 21:

1.　　 a; 2.b; 3.b; 4.a,b,c; 5.b,c; 6.a; 7.b,c; 8.c; 9.b; 10.a,b,c; 11.a,b,c; 12.b,c; 13.a;
14.　　 "Therefore I want you to know that God's salvation has been sent to the Gentiles, and they will listen!" (Acts. 28:28).

Lesson 22:

1.　　 He saw heaven opened and something like a large sheet being let down to earth by its four corners. It contained various four-footed animals, reptiles and birds.
2.　　 "Get up, Peter.  Kill and eat."
3.　　 No
4.　　 God instructed Peter not to call anything impure that God had made clean.
5.　　 3
6.　　 Although it was against Jewish law for Jews to associate or visit with Gentiles, no man should be considered or referred to as impure or unclean.
7.　　 The Holy Spirit fell upon the Gentiles.  They began speaking in tongues and were then baptized.
8.　　 "Therefore I want you to know that God's salvation has been sent to the Gentiles, and they will listen!" (Acts. 28:28).

Lesson 23:

1.　　 a,b; 2.b; 3.b; 4.a,b,c; 5.b,c; 6.a,b,c; 7.c; 8.c; 9.a,b; 10.b,c; 11.c;
12.　　 "Therefore I want you to know that God's salvation has been sent to the Gentiles, and they will listen!" (Acts. 28:28).

Lesson 24:

1.　　 T; 2.F; 3.T; 4.T; 5.T; 6.F; 7.T; 8.F;
9.　　 He considered his life worth nothing unless he finished the race and completed the task Jesus had given him, which was testifying to the Gospel of God's grace.
10.　　 T; 11.F; 12.T; 13.T; 14.T; 15.F; 16.T; 17.F; 18.T;
19.　　 "Therefore I want you to know that God's salvation has been sent to the Gentiles, and they will listen!" (Acts. 28:28).

Test 1: (Questions 1-20 worth 4.75; Question 21 worth 5 points.)

1.　　 Matthew, Mark, Luke, John and Acts
2.　　 They are referred to as the Pauline epistles because Paul wrote them.
3.　　 8
4.　　 Paul
5.　　 Revelation, John
6.　　 b; 7.a; 8.b; 9.b; 10.a; 11.F; 12.F; 13.T; 14.T; 15.F; 16.F; 17.T; 18.T; 19.T; 20.F;
21.　　 "For the Mighty One has done great things for me—holy is His name" (Luke 1:49).

Test 2: (Questions 1-20 worth 4.75; Question 21 worth 5 points.)

1.　　 He feared Jesus, King of the Jews, would dethrone him.
2.　　 the Magi
3.　　 Egypt
4.　　 He decreed that all baby boys 2 and under, living in and near Bethlehem be killed.
5.　　 Nazareth

6.      F; 7.F; 8.T; 9.T; 10.F; 11.F; 12.T; 13.F; 14.T; 15.F;
16-17.  He led Jesus into the desert to be tempted by Satan.
18.     3
19.     God's Word
20.     angels
21.     "And Jesus grew in wisdom and stature, and in favor with God and men" (Luke 2:52).

Test 3: (Questions 1-20 worth 4.75; Question 21 worth 5 points.)

1.      The Parable of the Sower
2-4.    Those who did not understand the Word; those who were not grounded in the Word; those who were focused on life's worries or the desire for wealth instead of the Word;
5.      John
6.      a; 7.b; 8.a,b,c; 9.c;10.b; 11.T; 12.T; 13.T; 14.F; 15.F; 16.F; 17.T; 18.F; 19.F; 20.T;
21.     "The King will reply, 'I tell you the truth, whatever you did for one of the least of these brothers of mine, you did for me'" (Matthew 25:40).

Test 4: (Questions 1-20 worth 4.75; Question 21 worth 5 points.)

1-3.    Peter, James, John
4.      3
5.      a kiss
6.      b; 7.a; 8.a; 9.c; 10.c; 11.F; 12.T; 13.F; 14.T; 15.T; 16.T; 17.F; 18.T; 19. F; 20.F;
21.     "For God did not send his Son into the world to condemn the world, but to save the world through him" (John 3:17).

Test 5: (Questions 1-20 worth 4.75; Question 21 worth 5 points.)

1-2.    Ananias and Sapphira
3.      Satan
4.      They fell over and died.
5.      All are sin and lead to destruction and, possibly, death.
6.      b; 7.a; 8.a, b; 9.c; 10.a; 11.T; 12.F; 13.T; 14.T; 15.T; 16.F; 17.T; 18.T; 19.F; 20.F;
21.     "Therefore go and make disciples of all nations, baptizing them in the name of the Father and of the Son and of the Holy Spirit and teaching them to obey everything I have commanded you" (Matthew 28:19-20a).

Test 6: (Questions 1-20 worth 4.75; Question 21 worth 5 points.)

1-2.    Paul & Silas
3.      praying and singing hymns to God
4.      An earthquake shook the prison.
5.      The jailer and his family got saved.
6.      c; 7.a; 8.a,c; 9.b; 10.a,b; 11.F; 12.F; 13.T; 14.T; 15.F; 16.T; 17.F; 18.T; 19.F; 20.F;
21.     "Therefore I want you to know that God's salvation has been sent to the Gentiles, and they will listen!" (Acts 28:28).

# NOTES